In the circle
of life - you
are a precious
Guide

♡

Kay

WHEEL OF LIFE CYCLES:

THE POWER OF LOVE TO HEAL YOUR LIFE

Kay Snow-Davis

S A G E   P U B L I S H E R S

Kapa`a, Kau`ai, Hawai`i, USA

Published in USA in 2006 by Sage Publishers
Kapa`a, Kau`ai, Hawai`i

Cover design by Cynthia Madden

ISBN 0-9771951-1-2

ENDORSEMENTS

"Kay Snow-Davis has developed a unique system to help us understand that our lives definitely move through 30-year cycles, and that each time we move through a cycle, we approach it with all the experiences we have accumulated to that point. And then we can move through that period from the more mature perspective of the new person we have become. If you spend some time to fully understand her system, your life and your relationships will flow so much more smoothly! I highly recommend it to you!!"

Heather Clarke, Arizona Enlightenment Center, Goodyear AZ

"In Wheel of Life Cycles, Kay Snow-Davis provides a highly differentiated system for navigating the spiraling challenges of our evolution as a species, as it is recapitulated in us as individuals through the stages of our development. It offers a life span developmental model that addresses our whole human potential- with its many facets."

Risa Kaparo, Ph.D. Poet, Performance Artist and Developer of Somatic Learning

"This material is strikingly valuable in helping to understand and align with your soul's plan. Using the Wheel of Life Cycles has made it possible for me to know the direction my life is taking and how to be present with that movement rather than try to force myself to do things that would only create blockages and frustration. It has also extremely helpful in working with others. By knowing where they are in their Life Cycle it has explained the lack of interest in a mate, co-workers and others for certain projects. This is good to know about. EXCELLENT."

Suzanne Franzen, Master Avatar Wizard

"I have known Kay Snow-Davis since 1993. She has been a friend first and foremost, and she has also been a consoler, and an educator. During the years I've known Kay; I have experienced major depression, severe side affects from PTSD, and an anxiety disorder. WOLC and her depth of knowledge has guided me in dealing with how the past affects my present life and my future.

WOLC also provided guidelines and tools I could use to change the way I was thinking and understand myself in a new way that supported my recovery. In the Wheel of Life Cycles, Kay explains in perfect detail how life experiences can influence how we think about ourselves and others who affect our life. She explains how we can overcome experiences that have left us scared and hurt. More importantly, Kay describes how we can fill in the blanks for parts of our life that were incomplete in the developmental process. The Wheel of Life Cycles will help you, as it has helped me, to better understand yourself both today and into the future. For people wanting to overcome the past and learn from it so you can move on to the present and future; Wheel of Life Cycles is a must read."

Lorie Tola, Atlanta GA

"Wheel of Life Cycles is a powerful lens, which allows us to objectively view our life, our relationships and life's contents from a wider impartial context. For those who are willing, the material continues to grow and expand meeting emergent awareness with expanding consciousness. Opening us to worlds upon worlds as we see our selves and others through our similarities in life's cycles rather than separate parts of creation. WOLC is a must for anyone who wishes to see and know him or herself more fully, for those wishing to understand their children, and for anyone in relationship. I believe the world today is ready, in fact ripe, for this tool and the wonderful unfolding potential for creative discovery and emergence it holds."

Jacquie Donahue, Artist, Mother, Wife

"After absorbing Kay Snow-Davis' work, adding it to my thinking, and then applying it to my parenting and teaching, I see that my relationships are transformed. Kay's Wheel of Life Cycles adds another piece of the puzzle to show us that life is less unpredictable and more simply beautiful than we might have thought. I love Kay's positive and strength-based approach to being here on this earth!"

Carrie Reuning-Humme,l Home schooling Mom, Suzuki Violin Teacher and Teacher
Trainer, Parenting Educator, and Certified Ppractitioner of Point of Power, Ithaca, NY

"From the first moment I heard the Wheel of Life Cycle information, I was changed. As I placed the events of my life into the Wheel I could see how the experiences supported me more than I ever realized - even the ones I thought were negative or bad. Insights continue to this day whenever I review the Cycles. Thank you, Kay, for another major gift from the heart."

Nanci Wesling Founder of Featherhawk Essences

DEDICATION

I dedicate this book to Y O U

and your courage to live,

no matter what!

Gratitude and Appreciation

For my personal journey through the Wheel of Life Cycles

My children, Christine, Mark and Joshua for being who you are,

And for your love and support

My sweet grandchildren, Rachel and Justin,

a gateway to the future

Raymond Borchers, my Heart Buddy and financial investor

Susan Clair for original editing

Hal Zina Bennett for the midwife editing

Heather Clarke for content editing

Sharon Gonsalves for final editing

Cynthia Madden for production management and illustrations

Vicki Wharton for original illustrations

Charles Davis for photographs

Ben Grisso graphic artist

Bill Gladstone for recognizing and supporting my work for many years

And

To You

My Beloved `Ohana (family) for loving me and being

In my life in all the ways that you are

Table of Contents

Forward

Just as fall turns into winter and summer is destined to follow spring, we share similar cycles within our lives that create our makeup as human beings.

In Wheel of Life Cycles, author Kay Snow-Davis, teaches that the secret to life is to learn from these cycles rather than to fight against them.

Instead of swimming against the current, Kay advocates going with the flow, seeing where it takes us, and then venturing back onto shore after the tide has settled. She encourages us to embrace life's cycles and learn from each experience while preparing ourselves for the next.

Within the pages of this beautifully written book, Kay offers credible examples and simple suggestions to help us discover our own wheel of life. Her easy-to-follow "baby step" system focuses on Golden Rule principles we can use to raise ourselves from where we are to where we want to be. Most important, she simplifies life's cycles into small, bite-size, "Aha" moments.

For example, remember the first time we fell in "puppy" love. Who doesn't recall that emotional roller coaster, with all its drama and chaos?

Although it was more than likely just a case of infatuation, we didn't know that at the time. Later, as more mature adults, we brought that knowledge and experience into our relationships and approached them with a different outlook and expectations. We could even offer the benefit of our experience to someone younger than ourselves.

We've heard the old adages a thousand times: "If I knew then, what I know now" or, "everything old is new again" or the best one ever, "what goes around comes around".

What do these sayings really mean?

They're trying to tell us that everything comes in cycles, and everything that ends has a new beginning. In this little gem of a book, Kay Snow-Davis offers insights to help us recognize life's events for what they are and as great precursors of what's about to come our way.

Wheel Of Life Cycles is almost like having your own crystal ball, but rather than being based on prediction, Ms. Snow-Davis' wisdom is based on years of experience and recognizing life's trends.

I dare you to read through these pages and not have more than one moment of wonder where you catch yourself asking, "How did she know that?" Once you consume this powerful system, you too will be armed with the knowledge to cope with your issues from the past and plan a course for your days, years, and life ahead.

Gregory Scott Reid

#1 Best-Selling Author, Speaker, and CEO of The Millionaire Mentor, Inc.

Introduction

Would you like a "second chance" at life? This book is for you. The life you have lived since you were born influences everything you do today. There are many experiences that got recorded into your cellular memory, your unconsciousness, and they continue to silently play out in your daily life, undetected and undirected by your conscious mind until you put in a new program. *Wheel of Life Cycles* helps fill in some of the missing pieces of your childhood by providing you with a conscious review, reflected through the eyes of your soul, allowing you to recognize the "life movie" you have been *starring* in up to now.

It is never too late to restructure your life foundation. You can recreate your past by changing the imprints of your life experiences. This will support your releasing your pain, fears, trauma, resentments, emptiness, and sadness. From these releases you can begin to experience your eternal love and joy waiting to emerge and become a part of your life today. *What you can feel you can heal. What you can recognize you can direct.*

To redirect your life, you need to develop new ways to respond to your reality and create options for the changes you want to make. Knowledge and awareness are keys. If you do not know there is another way of thinking and behaving, you cannot use it as an option. You create your future with the choices you make today. Without healthy adults and families making different choices in their own lives, our children's future will be a repeat of our ancestors' past.

There are many gifts and blessings from our ancestors and there are many challenges and limitations. We need to know the difference and choose differently to make a safe and loving world for all life.

An ancient tribal proverb says, "It takes a village to raise a child." Now is the time for us, as adults, to unite as a team and commit to healing our own lives so our children have role models who can demonstrate what healthy, balanced, caring, and respectful living looks like.

As a practitioner of Soul Purpose Astrology for over 35 years, I have learned to look at life in cycles and patterns and have a greater understanding of life and how our belief systems influence our choices. Life is ever evolving. The *Wheel Of Life Cycles*, a continuous spiral of life events, provides a unique view of how you grew up and how you can use your life experiences as stepping-stones for excellence rather than stumbling blocks that sabotage your future.

Quantum physics recognizes that all life is interconnected. The basic principle of science is relating. You are in relationship with every thing on this planet. Everyone's win is everyone's win. The more you can know of your connectedness to others, and all life, the greater possibility you have of investing your life in choices that create the results you desire.

Wheel Of Life Cycles is an original work received in 1987, and is a companion and compliment to the book, *Point Of Power*, *A Relationship With Your Soul* by Kay Snow-Davis, first edition published in 1995. The information in *Wheel Of Life Cycles* is very comprehensive in providing insights and information about the cycles of your life. By reviewing the cycles, at any age, you get a greater understanding of how your beliefs, attitudes, and behaviors have been influenced by your life experiences and you can gain a new perception of the experiences, and create the desired change you want.

Wheel Of Life Cycles offers a safe and gentle means for consciously restructuring your belief system by providing another perception of your past. This view does not evoke the same emotional response as the originating incident. When you can take one step away from your own pain and trauma of life, you can allow your mind to receive insights from your heart and soul that sustain and support your movement in life in a different way.

Everyone on this planet is doing the best they know how, based on the events, circumstances, conditions and people that influenced and molded their realities.

Your Presence makes a difference in life. Consciously make a difference by co-creating a world where *you* know –

I AM SAFE, I AM LOVED, I AM WANTED.

Blessings to you,

Kay

Guidelines

You may want to purchase a journal and record your insights as you go through your cycles of life. After you review a cycle and explore the questions, take time to journal your personal awareness and thoughts that you are discovering.

When you make a conscious life change, take at least one step of action to anchor in your new decision and commitment.

All creativity includes these steps:

- Receive
- Conceive
- Gestate
- Deliver.

Accept yourself just as you are. Start where you are with what you have and more will be given.

WHEEL OF LIFE

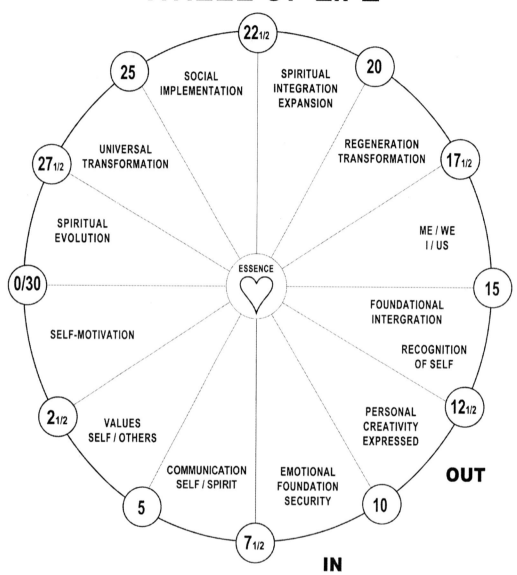

Illustration: Wheel of Life Cycles

The Wheel Of Life represents each 2½-year cycle that you go through in your stages of development. The first 15 years you are building your life foundation, mentally and emotionally. From 15 to 30 years old you begin to create life experiences based on that original foundation. Each cycle, after 15 years, is always influenced by the cycle directly opposite on the wheel.

For example, 15 – 17½ is influenced by the cycle from birth to 2 ½ even though those beliefs or habits were developed unconsciously they will still influence your personal relating needs and desires throughout your life and will be very impactful during the 15 -17 ½ cycle.

This helps you recognize that all life experiences influence the overall balance and expression in your life; there are no isolated incidents in your life. Everything is recorded in your cellular memory and will play out at some time or another, based on the incidents that trigger that memory.

It takes 30 years to complete one full cycle. Then you begin the Wheel Of Life Cycles again. You will participate in the cycles again at age 30, 60 or 90, each time fortified with your life experiences and able to consciously re-direct any cycle of your life by the choices you make as you go through it again. It is never too late to restructure your life foundation.

Chapter 1

How to Use the Cycle Information

Welcome to an exciting, revealing journey of your life using the Wheel of Life Cycles. There are many ways to use this material. I will give you an overview so as you read the book you will have the opportunity to create a revised life foundation that will enrich your appreciation of you and your journey.

The value of using and understanding your life cycles has been demonstrated over and over in my clients' lives during the years. One of the most significant is a family of four that I have participated with for about 20 years. The four family members are in consecutive cycles, so for about 2 years everything goes along pretty well and then chaos sets in. As we worked with this pattern, we discovered that every 2 - 2½ years each member changed cycles. There was always about a 6-month time frame where everyone was adjusting to their own changes as well as the whole focus of the family dynamics being rearranged requiring adjustment within the family unit.

After we discovered this, their level of stress was reduced and living together as a family seemed much more manageable because they knew why this chaos kept coming up over and over and what to do to make it different for themselves and each other. The more you understand your family dynamics and recognize that you can influence change for yourself, the safer you can feel in your life.

In today's changing world, your home is your sanctuary, and if it is filled with chaos this dramatically influences your stress level and your sense of well-being. The collective stress level is directly connected to personal safety and our sense of safety as a global family.

CYCLE INFORMATION

For everything there is a time, there is a season. This basic principle of physics applies in our human experience as well. The difference is that we are not taught about our human cycles in the same way we are taught about the tides, the seasons, the solstice, etc. When you begin to look at your life in cycles, your reality becomes more congruent and compatible with the universe you live in. We humans are subject to the universal laws of life on this planet: gravity, seasons, oxygen transfer, transmutation, assimilation, etc. The more we can become aware of this universal plan and accept and allow our life to develop in a more natural way, the more we can accept and experience grace, peace and personal fulfillment - mentally, physically, emotionally and spiritually. These are some of the ways you can use the cycle information in *Wheel Of Life Cycles*:

First Thirty-Year Cycle   **Birth to 30 years**

- **Foundation** - many people academically graduate from "school" at 18. You may continue your education and have other forms of graduation throughout your life. Every thirty years in the "school of life" you enter a major time of new beginnings. From birth to 15 years old you are creating the foundation that you will use and build on the rest of your life. From 15 to 30 years of age, you have life experiences that assist you in consciously recognizing what kind of foundation you are developing. Some of this recognition comes from challenges in life and some from the blessings of life. Both represent the reality of a balanced life and your ability to recognize your strength to meet any life experience and to grow and learn from it.

Second Thirty-Year Cycle   **30 years to 60-years**

- **Implementation** - another chance. . . .a new beginning at age 30. You are at the door of life once again, this time with 30 years of living experiences so you will not enter this door of life in the same way you did at birth. You can consciously choose now how you will restructure your original life foundation created from birth to 15 years old as you re-enter this foundational cycle from 30 to 45 years. There is plenty of time to review and restructure this next 15 years of your life. Your personal power is strengthened daily when you live your life one day at a time and make choices that are consciously congruent with what is happening right now, not in reaction to what you experienced in your past at any age. The choices you use to expand and change your foundational beliefs and emotions from 30 to 45 will be the resources and guiding force for your life from 45 to 60-years old.

Third Thirty-Year Cycle　　　　　　**60-years to 90 years**

- **Spiritual -** you have had 60-years experience in this "life school" and nothing appears the same as it did when you were born or at 30 years old. Many desires and passions of life that were motivating forces for you from 30 to 60-years of age do not have the same impact in your life anymore. Your perception of life could be more narrow or broader, depending on your ability to trust yourself, the universe you live in and your courage to take steps of action according to your heart and soul commitments. During this cycle your focus will be called to return to the big picture of life, your primary relationship with your soul which experiences beauty, passion, power and wisdom by being a part of the "big picture," rather than just talking about it. You have the ability and experience to recognize the attributes that constitute quality living and what is really enduring.

Fourth Thirty-Year Cycle　　　　　　**90 years into forever**

- **Divine Wisdom -** at the age of 90, entering this thirty-year cycle for the fourth time, longevity itself is a major and admirable quality of life. People are curious and interested in what you think. They want to know about your history. Your life is intriguing to them because your vantage point in life spans such a long time and has involved many changes, including inventions that may have occurred before they were even born. The veil gets thinner and thinner during this cycle and it is easier to be a part of the spiritual world and still be in a body. Since your personal willfulness has had many years of expression, your willingness to receive Spirit gracefully and allow your innate wisdom to come through you is fulfilling and gratifying for you and those who are blessed to receive what you share.

CYCLES OF RENEWAL

In this school of life, you have key turning points where you can review your life and recognize that the choices made at these specific times carried a lasting influence, sometimes life long.

Significant times of change occur for you around:

•	7½ years	15 years	22½ years	30 years
•	37½ years	45 years	52½ years	60-years
•	67½ years	75 years	82½ years	90 years

Every time you come to these aspects of time, whether it is your age or your marriage or your business, you will have significant choices to make that will have lasting affects on your life.

Think about the questions that arise from many people when someone divorces after 22 or 30 years of marriage. Some people cannot understand why this would happen after all these years. When you begin to recognize life and changes through cycles, the number of years is not as significant as the choices that are made at these significant times.

These cycles are times in your life, partnerships, businesses, organizations, etc., when evaluating your choices and changing your lifestyle alters your course in life in order to continue to expand your soul purpose. Sometimes the choice is made consciously, sometimes unconsciously, driven by your heart and soul. Your conscious mind may be surprised or shocked by the options that you never have considered as part of " the plan" in your life.

Sometimes the changes feel wonderful and sometimes they feel awful. How these changes feel to you is not nearly as important as what you choose to do with these changes when they occur. These cycles are major demarcation points in your life. If you were raised in an indigenous tribe these times of change would be celebrated as rites of passage so you could consciously use the life changes to empower your growth and movement.

In our "civilized" world, we have been educated to change our focus from cycles in life to analysis and linear thinking. We have lost contact with the guiding principles of the universal cycles.

Everything you do, every day, influences your life. You can use these everyday experiences and become conscious of your thinking and make your life a natural rite of passage. When you brush your teeth, be conscious of your thinking, you can be in gratitude for this moment – you have teeth to brush, you have water to use, you have a bathroom to brush you teeth in, etc.

Participating in your daily life with a conscious mind and grateful heart supports your creating life experiences in a more gracious and manageable way.

WHEEL OF LIFE

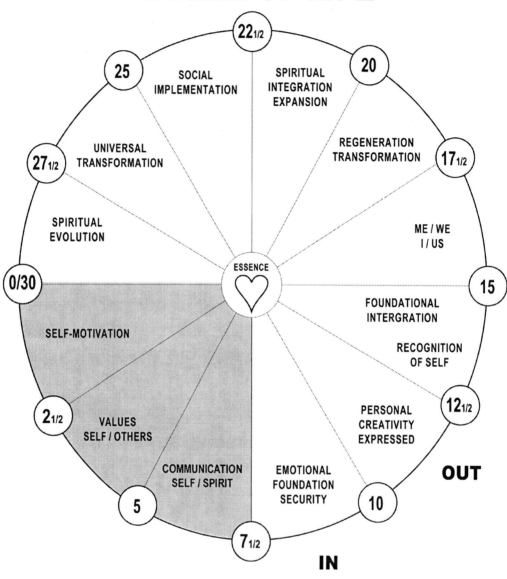

Illustration: 7 ½ Year Cycle

Review of these special cycles of change:

- The individual cycle, at age 7½, 37½, 67½ is to stabilize your life emotionally so you can become more intimate with your own feelings and desires. During this cycle you begin to recognize your feelings and emotions that may be different than anyone else in your family. This cycle is when you begin to question your inner desires and feelings based on what the "outer" family experiences may be.

- The 7½, 37½, 67½ - year cycle for marriages, business, and organizations use the same basic principle as the individual cycle. This is a time of decision, recognition and the need to expand the foundation of the marriage, business or organization. When a marriage, business or organization reaches this cycle, it is ready for expansion on many levels; and if the participants are flexible and open, it does not necessitate the demise of the structure, simply the expansion of it and everyone involved.

Whatever lifestyle or structure has suited the conditions of these experiences until now must expand and accommodate the pending growth that life offers. Everything on the planet is subject to change and expansion as a continuum in life.

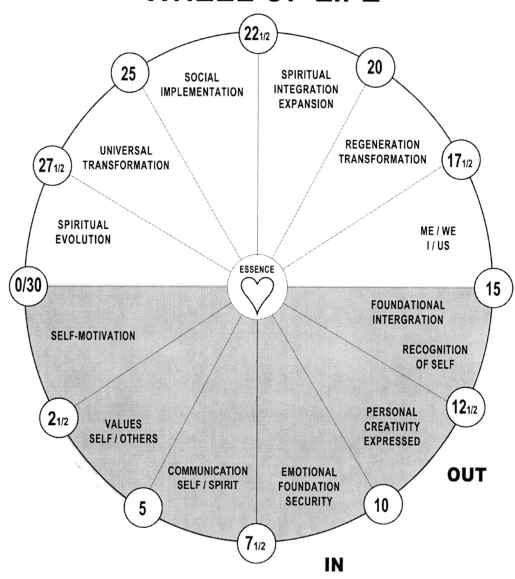

Illustration: 15-year Cycle

- At age 15, 45, 75 the childhood foundation you have experienced from birth is your preparation for the exposure and expansion you are going to have particularly in the next 15 years of your life. Through your experiences from birth, you weave the threads of your life together to use them, consciously or unconsciously, in the choices you make each day. This provides the option of increasing your strength of character, esteem and confidence that you rely on to carry you through your life cycles until you are 30.

- The 15, 45, 75-year cycle in marriages, businesses, and organizations is a strong cycle of challenge and change. If these structures made it through the 7½-year cycles by opening and expanding together, they need to use that stability and meet this cycle with a commitment to make whatever changes are necessary for the next 15 years together. The commitments being made now need to have a greater depth and trust level to provide enthusiasm, inspiration and vision for the increased power that is available at this time in marriage, business, and organization. The level of relating in the partnerships has been tested in many ways, and it is time to take that strength forward and expand the marriage, business and organization by conscious choices that support everyone participating.

True acceptance of who you are, where you are in life and where your desires and visions are focused will have a strong influence on this next 7 ½ years of your personal life or the life of the marriage, business or organization.

WHEEL OF LIFE

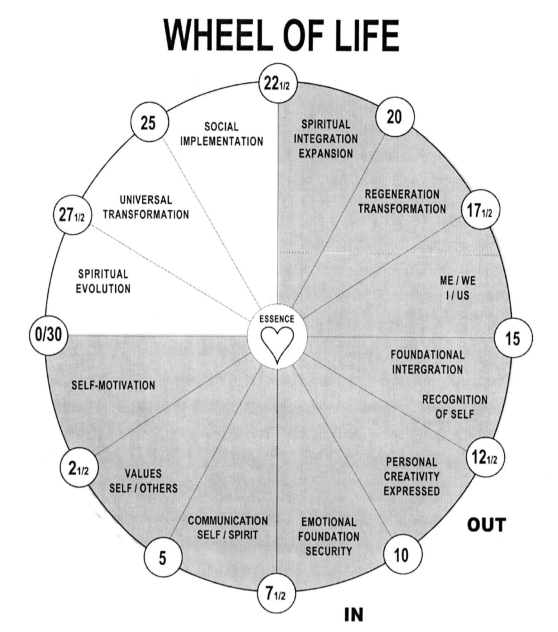

Illustration: 22-½ Year Cycle

- Personally arriving at the cycle of 22½, 52½, 82½ is the time to recognize and claim your core values so you are ready to express your life through your work/profession/career with integrity and stability. This is a strong "graduation," because it is now time to expose your beliefs, attitudes and behavior to the public, through your profession or your lifestyle. This may require a lot of exposure, and your confidence is dependent on your emotional foundation developed during your first cycle from 7½ - 10.

- For marriages, businesses and organizations, this cycle calls everything to "front and center." There is no place to hide when this cycle comes up. Whatever has been hidden, denied, unclear, unethical, limited, confused or suppressed will come to the surface now and must be cleared before the marriage, business or organization can continue.

This is a true test of re-committing on every level. The strength of the spiritual foundation at this time influences the possibility of meeting this test and being strengthened for the next cycle.

WHEEL OF LIFE

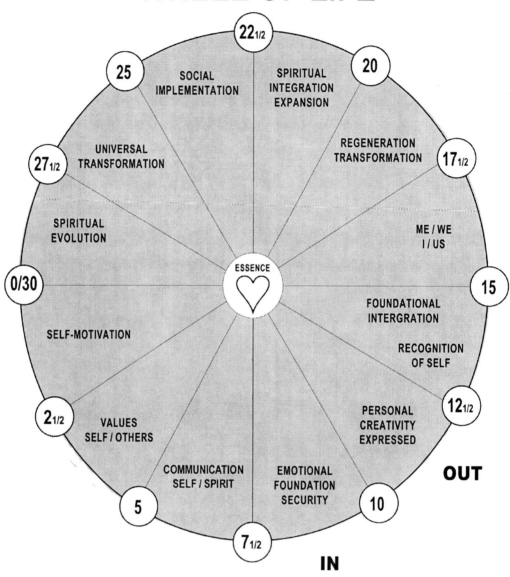

Illustration: 30-year Cycle

- The 30, 60, 90-year demarcation is time for a new birth. Your life now has 30 years of physical, mental, emotional and spiritual experience that were not available before.

- By examining the experiences of your past to decide whether you want to continue, modify, eliminate or re-direct your beliefs and lifestyle, you give focus and direction to your intention for the next 30 years.

  The strength of your self-identity will influence all your choices. "Who am I?" is a really good question to ask in order to begin restructuring your foundation in life. Knowing who you really are will enhance your choices to create fulfillment, success, joy and a sense of purpose and accomplishment in the next 30-year cycle.

- For marriages, businesses, and organizations, this cycle is truly a new beginning. If you made it this far by being conscious of your choices, direction and interactions, there is a good possibility you have created an enduring foundation that is ready to create "new life" and continue to meet the challenges of change in a cohesive way. There is no way the next 30 years will be like the first 30, so a new plan needs to come into action.

CYCLE AWARENESS

Marriages   Families   Personal   Partners   Business   Organizations

The *Wheel Of Life Cycles* is very effective in increasing personal awareness of each individual's cycle and the awareness of family and group dynamics through the cycles. When you know what cycle your life is in, you can participate consciously in creating the support you need to naturally grow stronger and learn how to cooperate with others in a balanced and healthy way.

Cycle awareness assists in reducing the judgments you may have of yourself and others who are not living their life "your way." Besides being a separate individual from you, they may be in a very different cycle than yours.

The cycle awareness applies whether it is for an individual, couple, family, business, organization or nation. You are universally united through the cycles of life and the more conscious you are of this interconnection, the more you can "take your place" in the divine plan of creation and contribute your gifts with less stress, struggle, conflict and harm to all life.

Chapter 2

Your Personal Journey with the Cycles of Life

In the movie of your life, you are the star, the main character; therefore, the only experience you can have of your "life movie" is from the inside out, the way you see and experience your reality. This is the basis we all have for defining the way we relate to everything in life. It is important to know that no one on the planet has your same fingerprints, your DNA or your teeth. No one on the planet has your same life experience or reality base. Knowing this can reduce your expectations and judgments of yourself and others and increase your compassion and recognition for what an amazing journey humans are on to learn to co-habitate on this home planet with respect and reverence for all life.

Using the *Wheel Of Life Cycles* gives you another view of your life and allows you to rearrange your experience by seeing these life situations with a new set of eyes and allowing the experience to be renewed and restructured to support your life now. And the wonderful part is, you get to go through these cycles more than once, just in case you missed something the first or even the second time around.

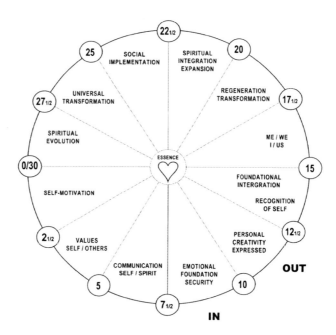

When you use the Wheel of Life Cycles for your own movie review, it is pretty straightforward. You can look at the cycle you are in now, determined by your age, and see what the focus is for this cycle. Then if you look at Illustration above, check the cycle right across the wheel and see what the power and focus is for that cycle. After 15 years old, no matter what your age, you will always be living from the influence of the foundational cycles developed from birth to 15 years old as well as the current cycle you are in. Whether you are just reviewing cycles for yourself or want to review cycles for your partner, children, parents, neighbors or anyone else, the technique is the same.

Please remember as you review these cycles that the words that I have used for the information are my words, my opinion and are meant to activate your ideas and your opinions about yourself and your experience. Do not use these cycles to describe or identify yourself, but merely to help you recognize other possibilities about yourself that you may not have thought of or were unable to recognize at the time of your experience.

As a human being, you are on a journey. Life is not a destination. The fullness of any given moment in your life is dependent on your ability to be fully present with your experience and not "coloring it" with your past or your expectations of the future. I think this is a life-long adventure to just practice being fully present. You can enjoy this journey a lot more if you drop your judgments and expectations of yourself and others and begin to participate in life as an adventure of continuous change. Any adventure in life is filled with all kinds of feelings and experiences so if you participate in your life as an adventure, expect the same thing. Something is always going on, changing, happening, interfering with your well thought out plan -- that is truly life, ever changing. Expect the unexpected and meet and manage the moment as it occurs.

Your resistance or comfort with change will determine the quality of your journey. If change is particularly challenging for you, especially sudden changes, life is probably an adventure filled with a lot of stress. If change is exciting for you, you may feel really blessed in life because everything is changing so fast. If you like change in moderation, a little bit at a time, you may have moments of feeling fulfilled and peaceful and moments of feeling very challenged and stressed. On this adventure, we are all seeking balance to increase the quality of our life by feeling safe, loved and wanted. Resiliency is a key component to finding balance. Being as flexible as you can with life changes allows the power of resiliency to support your intention to create balance. Enjoy your journey through the *Wheel Of Life Cycles*.

Chapter 3

Recognize the Power of Cycles in Business & Organizations

Everything in life has a beginning. When you use the *Wheel Of Life Cycles* to look at the cycle your marriage, business or organization is in, you use the date of your marriage or the starting date for your organization or business as the zero or birth cycle. On the *Wheel Of Life Cycles* start at zero and move forward through the years the same as you would for an individual. Whatever the "age" of the marriage, business or organization is the cycle the entity is in. From here on we will refer to these three as the entity. Everything is energy and information and when you structure energy and information in a format of marriage, business or an organization, it truly has a life of its own and the participants act as the cells of the entity, everyone contributing to the whole, the entity.

We all breathe the same breath; we all receive life through our food from the earth we live on. We are interconnected as energy and information through the breath and the life force on this planet. You may or may not have this as your belief and it really doesn't matter. Before gravity had a name, it was influencing our lives, so it is with energy and information. We are kindergartners as humans understanding what life as energy really means. Using *Wheel Of Life Cycles* gives you another window for your personal and professional reality and how we influence each other as energy and information.

For example, if your marriage is 4 years old, then you are in the cycle of 2½ to 5 years old. For an individual this is the cycle of creating values, quality in life and influencing self-esteem and self-confidence. Taking these same principles you would apply this to the entity, enlarging your perception from a personal view to a larger more collective view. In this case, the marriage would be in the cycle of consciously establishing the foundational values and qualities that are desired or reflected in this marriage by the two partners participating. Clarity and unity developed in this cycle will determine the strength and resiliency of the marriage for years to come.

This cycle is very important for all entities. Without a solid foundation on values and quality of life, the older the entity gets the more the split or conflicted values will show up as resistance or vulnerability in the entity and the participants. The places where we feel vulnerable, personally or professionally, are the places we "protect" ourselves, rather than "expose" ourselves for greater learning. Once we begin to establish protection patterns versus learning patterns, we are creating separation rather than unity. The divine order of the Universe always calls us to a greater level of balance and strength if we are willing to listen and be guided.

Conflict is a messenger that reflects that something is not harmonious, congruent or in integrity, personally or professionally. If we have the courage to choose "openness to learning" rather than positioning ourselves "to defend," we can use conflict as a red flag notifying us that something is "off." Then we can use conflict as a support for making course corrections in our choices and focus on creating unity instead of separation. Unity is an experience, not an understanding in the mind.

The entity is its own expression of life, the same as a baby. A baby has a mother and a father as contributors to its life expression and yet a child is its own unique expression in life, just as their finger prints demonstrate: there is no one on this planet quite like this baby, even if it is a multiple birth. So it is with your marriage, business or organization. No matter whom the contributing partners are this entity becomes its own life expression influenced by the input and behavior of those participating with the entity.

Whether I work with an individual, families, or any entity - marriage, business or organization there are some basic principles that apply. Everything has a core essence, which I see the same as DNA in the human cell. This is the receiving and distributing point for all energy and information. The DNA of our human body is a magnetic center for exchange with the life force through the breath. Each individual in a marriage, business, or organization is a DNA, a magnetic field for receiving life and exchanging life with the entity/world. Every cell counts in our physical body to create wellness. Every person counts in an entity to create wellness and balance.

This is the reason you can use the *Wheel of Life Cycles* personally and professionally. There is no difference, only the numbers involved and the structure.

Another aspect that is available when you know the cycle of the entity, then you can add in the information for the individuals involved with the entity and get even a greater awareness of the energy and information that is available for creation at any given time. If your marriage is 4 years old and in the 2½ - 5 year cycle, then you check out your personal cycle for yourself and your partner and know that your personal cycles are also contributing to this marriage entity, whether you are conscious of this or not. Life is a magical, divine puzzle and it is expressed on so many levels that we do not consciously understand or know, and yet daily these "unknowns" contribute to the quality of life we live.

These are just a few examples of some ways that you can use *Wheel of Life Cycles* to see your life through another window of awareness. I know you will discover your very own portals of movement and awareness as you journey your *Wheel of Life Cycles*. The main thing, have fun and be committed to create more and more joy in your life, which is the doorway to your Soul.

Foundation

First 30 Year Cycle

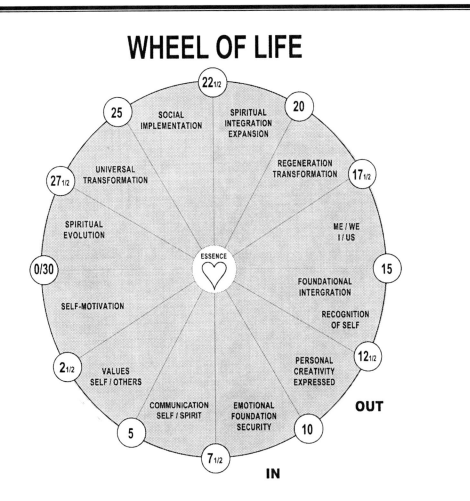

WHEEL OF LIFE

Birth to 30 years

School and learning are a life-long process in this University of Life. Every thirty years in the school of life you enter a major time of new beginnings. The first thirty-year cycle provides the foundation that you will use and build on the rest of your life.

Birth to 2½ Years

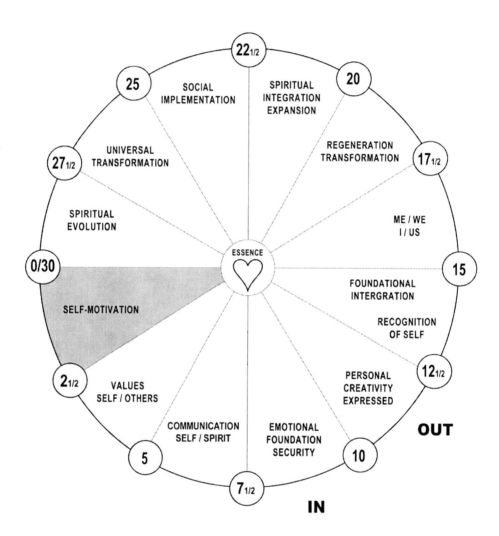

THEME

Attention
  Survival
Motivation
  Personal Needs

24

Chapter 4

Attention and Motivation

POWER

One of your primary needs, as a human being, is attention. We are one of the species that must be supported, after our birth, in order to survive. Attention is a basic need for survival. Without attention you cannot get your needs met for food, shelter, clothing, nurturing as an infant and child. This cycle is where you unconsciously developed your motivational patterns for getting attention. It worked you are still here!

Developing your motivational patterns to get attention after birth was not a conscious process: it was a reactionary process created by the way you were treated by your caregivers and how you mentally, emotionally and physically experienced the environments in which you were being raised. Recognizing your primary motivational pattern is very powerful because you can consciously create attention-getting methods that meet your current needs in a balanced and healthy way.

Gaining awareness that attention is a primal need and recognizing what behavior you developed as an infant so you could get attention will provide a new awareness of how you are motivated today, in relating to others, in order to get the attention you want.

As you begin to recognize and explore some of your basic emotional imprints that create the behavioral patterns that affect your life as an adult, you can become conscious of their affect in your life, and with consciousness comes choice. You can decide if these imprints from early childhood contribute to your current desires and intentions or sabotage them. Having a conscious recognition of developed patterns of behavior puts you in the driver's seat of your daily choices and you can begin to make decisions that support who you are now and what you want in life.

VULNERABILITY

Attention means survival, especially as an infant and toddler and life requires that you go to any length or use any behaviors necessary to survive. The emotional imprints created to get attention as an infant will influence the rest of your life until you recognize and change them. Because your motivation to get attention is developed unconsciously during infancy, you have refined and sophisticated your behavior as you have grown up, yet the underlying pattern was developed from birth and has a foundational influence in the choices you make today to get your personal needs met.

Today's adult behaviors can be a mask for underlying needs that are not consciously recognized. Unless your behaviors match and represent what you are really feeling and seeking, you will feel split. You can recognize these splits when your action in life creates a reaction that is surprising to you, something other than what you intended. These events are good messengers to alert you to the possibility that you may be "thinking" one thing and "desiring" something different. This discovery takes some "tuning into your inner world" by listening to your heart and soul desires.

You could not filter out these impressions and influences as an infant because your conscious mind was not developed to act as a filter. This is why the cycles of life help reveal your inner movie script by revealing your hidden imprints through today's relationships. Once you have this information and awareness you can re-direct some of your energy, emotions, thoughts and behaviors so they can be updated and really represent your truth from your heart and soul. If you did not feel safe as an infant, your emotional needs probably were suppressed so your basic needs to be warm, fed, clothed, and sheltered were all that you received. This is not enough. Your life is more than just survival needs. We translate attention as love. If abuse is what you received as attention, then you may grow up and translate that love is abuse.

It is never too late to create and live a balanced healthy life. Your empty emotional spaces and deep heart's longings can be filled in your life even if they were missing for you as an infant or in your childhood. *What you can feel you can heal. What you can recognize you can direct.* Your willingness to see life differently and make different choices will create a different reality for you. Using the *Wheel of Life Cycles* will assist you in your journey to recover your submerged joy that eternally awaits your recognition and release.

DISCOVERIES

Take a moment to recall your early life, as far back as you can remember, or whatever you recall your family saying you did as a baby. You can begin to recognize what you had to do to get attention as an infant.

Did you have to cry or scream and holler?

Did you have to get sick?

Did you have to be still? Some or all of the above?

What did you have to do to get your needs met?

Unless you have consciously identified your original motivational behavior, and changed it, you are still seeking your attention in the similar methods you learned from birth to 2½, jus more subtle and sophisticated now than as an infant.

All life is subject to the universal laws of movement, change and space. The imprints held in your neurological system that got developed from birth to 2½ can be redirected any time in your life. The neurological system is not based on time so the imprints remain until they are neurologically cleared. From birth to 2½ years old, you were unconsciously establishing, your identity and relationship with yourself through survival needs which influences every thought you think, every attitude you develop and every behavior you display during your life until you can consciously redirect your energy.

Everything is energy and energy is always in motion and creation. As a soul, living in a human body, you are energy in motion. Whatever you can recognize you can direct or redirect. Whatever you can feel you can heal. The energy moving through you as an infant is the same energy available throughout your life. When you create a conscious relationship with your soul, you can consciously redirect your life, because you are energy in motion waiting to be directed by your conscious choices.

When you recognize the way you motivate yourself to get attention, and take responsibility for creating behaviors that are healthy and fulfilling for you, you have begun to make a major investment in the future for yourself and our children in the global family. Recognizing your empty spaces and filling them with healthy and responsible behaviors creates a sense of wholeness and fulfillment for you. This is the beginning of "walking your talk," having your inner world of your heart and soul match your outer life. You then become an authentic role model in life, especially for our children, influencing the foundational stability that every child, big and little, needs in order to feel safe, loved and wanted. Your actions speak louder than your words. Every thought, word, attitude and behavior is an investment in your future. Are you investing in what you want returned to you?

The basis of science now is that everything is energy and information relating to everything else, no matter what form or structure or whether it is demonstrating as trees, birds, ocean, flowers, wind, animals or people. We are all energy in motion and relating to every other form of life. This is called Oneness.

DIRECTIVES

We are all in recovery from some kind of wounding. I believe that a huge percent of hurt experienced by us as we are growing up is committed through innocence and ignorance. You model what you live and you pass on what you learn, consciously or unconsciously. If you are to have a different future you need to become conscious of your training, modeling and behavior and make current choices that are congruent with your personal truth. To assist this change you need a conscious relationship with your heart and soul; where your divine plan in life is recorded awaiting your recognition so you can recreate your life and experiences by recognizing you are much more than just a physical body.

You are a Universal Being living in a human body in order to express your soul plan, mentally, physically, emotionally and spiritually. Spirit, love, God, Nature, the Divine Plan, no matter what we call it, all life is united on this planet. Everything is linked to universal eternal life; many humans just don't consciously recognize and believe it yet.

As you go through the *Wheel of Life Cycles*, do so with great compassion and love for yourself and all those who have influenced you. Everyone, including you, has lived as consciously and as clearly as possible at any given moment based on their own life patterns and experiences. You are life in process, energy in motion, still being created. Everything is possible.

In most cases, you will not have a conscious memory of your life during this early cycle. As you review this time in your life now, you may remember and discover many experiences at this age that have deeply influenced your life today. You are a soul living through a human body in a human experience. Just as no one else on the planet has your fingerprints, or your DNA, no one else has your soul plan. It is as innate and ordained from the Divine, as are your fingerprints, just not as obvious or tangible.

We are all in this classroom of life together, learning and growing one day at a time as a global family. All life experiences are a blessing even though they may feel awful. We grow easiest through love, compassion, respect and patience with each other and ourselves. Since life is a process, not a "quick fix", giant leaps and baby steps occur in life. Let the unfolding of your soul be organic and naturally paced by your own divine plan and timing.

FOCUS

- **Trust**

  Learn to trust yourself, your desires and choices in life. You can have what you want and still be cooperative with others.

- **Self-referencing**

  You can choose your method of getting satisfying and fulfilling attention. You are not dependent on others to make that choice for you.

- **Acceptance**

  Accept the truth of who you are as an eternal soul, not only a human being. This releases your eternal power of love and gratitude in your life.

GUIDELINES & QUESTIONS

1. List three things you discovered about yourself reading this chapter.

2. How are these affecting you right now? How are you feeling about these discoveries?

3. Are you getting what you truly want in life? If not, why not?

4. Write a release letter to anyone that you still feel angry, betrayed, hurt, abandoned, or in resentment towards. Do not edit this letter and DO NOT SEND THIS LETTER. This release is for you. Burn this letter the same day written.

5. Continue to write release letters until you can feel compassion and forgiveness for your self and others.

6. List five qualities that you recognize you want to create in your life now to have a more fulfilling lifestyle.

2½ to 5 Years

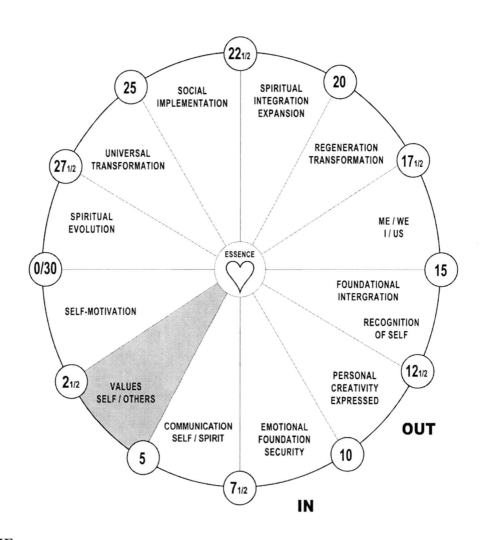

THEME

    Personal Value
        Values in life
    Self-recognition
        Sexuality

Chapter 5

Values

POWER

We all need to be seen heard and recognized throughout our life. The basis for your socialized value system was developed from 2½ to 5 years old. The primary influence learned at this age was how to behave to get the recognition and approval you were seeking. You were exposed to greater numbers of people and life conditions that taught you, by the response you received, whether your behavior and choices were acceptable, or not, in your family and social situations. Since the conscious mind at this stage of development was not an active filter as much as it was an active receiver, you were very impressionable.

Your sense of self-worth and confidence began to develop during this cycle and because your conscious mind was not developed to sort out your life experiences, your sorting mechanism was your feelings. Does this feel good or not? Innately you want your life to feel good. You want to feel safe and happy. It is a very basic level of living. Through social interactions you began to determine how to behave, how you were valued, or not, and how to value other people, their needs and possessions.

At this age you are physically developing and experiencing what your body is capable of doing. You learned to walk and then run, climb and many other adventures. Your coordination is getting stronger so your balance in your body is growing daily. Your vocabulary is increasing so you can communicate with more words. Your bladder is developing so you can actually begin to control your urination and possibly elimination as well. These first two cycles from birth to 5 years old are a defining time of beginning to recognize and use the capabilities of your physical body.

As a child, you live in Oneness with an innate knowing that every part of you and your body is sacred. Your body is a living temple, a mini universe that reflects the natural order of the Divine Plan. There is no part of you, your mind, body, emotions, or spirit that is your enemy. You are Divine, and there is a higher order always orchestrating the unity of life through you. Every part of you is designed to work in harmony with the universe, otherwise the air you breathe and the food you eat could not be transformed into essential elements for sustaining and renewing your physical life. In your naturalness, love and joy motivate you. These qualities never die in you; they simply get buried from experiences that modify your relationship with your naturalness.

VULNERABILITY

During this stage of your development you were very impressionable. Ninety plus percent of what you learned was from visual input and imprinted in your subconscious, influencing your self-esteem and your developing values. Through social interactions you began to determine how to behave, how you were valued, or not, and how to value other people, their needs and possessions. This was all done unconsciously because your conscious mind had not developed a filter system to make choices about what to bring in and what to reject. Subjectively, in order to get attention and approval, you may have chosen to submit to the socialized values you were taught or to attempt to do what felt natural for you, until the social response notified you this choice does not work. In life your unconscious is like a computer hard drive, whatever comes in is recorded at a cellular level and will affect your behavior until you can recognize and change that imprint. You can change cellular imprints through neurological clearings when you are conscious of it. (see www.emofree.com and www.universalhealthmethod.com)

What you can recognize you can direct.

What you can feel you can heal.

Your true value of life, and your relationship with your body was influenced at this stage of development through your environment and interaction with others. Your experiences at this age deeply affect your sense of self worth, confidence and safety in relating to others throughout your life. Your experience at this age and how you received attention/approval created a foundation for your social behavior. If you were supported in your behavior when you were seeking to get approval those behaviors were imprinted and became part of your method of relating to others in seeking to get your needs met. If you were not supported and your behavior was met with dramatic reactions or abuse, you could have developed withdrawn and introverted behavior or defiant and rebellious reactions to continue to get attention, depending on what response would get you the attention you needed. The motivation is the same: satisfying the need to get attention, even if it is harmful or disapproval.

When you get a negative response, rather than approval, your true self begins to hide, for safety's sake, and you may begin giving up and saying and doing what others want, so they will like you and hopefully not hurt or harass you. Your reality becomes conflicted when your inner voice and hearts desires do not match your outer performance in life. When this separation occurs, this deeply affects your sense of safety and trust of yourself, which in turn influences your trust level with others. You cannot feel safe when you are trying to satisfy two different value systems, such as your inner truth and desires and society's demands and expectations of you.

DISCOVERIES

As you become more conscious of your programming that was created during this cycle and you decide you want to revise some of that programming, it is important to sort out what values you learned to believe in and what values belong to your heart and soul. You may be surprised to discover that what you *think* your values are may be very different from your *true* values when you begin to examine them.

The true value in life is activated from your innate relationship with your soul. The illusions that you believe about yourself and others are learned and repeated through your conscious mind. Your conscious mind may have been influenced and trained with judgments and conditions throughout your life experiences, and these experiences influence the recognition you have of your purpose and value in life. Since birth, all input influences your behavior and developing beliefs.

As other's value systems were imposed upon you, you learned to doubt your natural abilities and responses to life, deferring to those who had a dominant influence in your life even though they had a different value system than your heart and soul. Since attention and approval are primary needs, especially at this age, you try to adjust your life and behavior to accommodate the requirements of those adults in your immediate world, especially your primary caregivers. This sets in motion self-doubt created when you feel one thing and are told it is not true and given someone's version of their truth that does not match what you feel. This creates an inner conflict, because your heart says one thing and your mind learns to behave or respond in another way in order to feel safe and get attention and approval. This creates a split in your reality base and a sense of distrust of your inner feelings and desires.

During this time frame, as you are developing a relationship with others, you are developing an active relationship with your body's skills and functions. Usually at this age is when you get "potty trained". The method, words, attitude, acceptance, or rejection that you experienced as you were being potty trained, taught you how to relate to your bodily functions and your genitals. This training influences your relationship with the reproductive areas of your body and created a foundational response that influences your sexuality on a subliminal level. If your experience was one of encouragement, patience, support and caring, you could naturally have a higher regard for your genitals and your natural body functions. If you received the message that "this part of your body" was acceptable and wonderful just as any other part of your body, then your relationship with your sexuality had a much better chance of being healthy and natural rather than feeling unhealthy and needing to be hidden.

If your experience was one of harassment, control, punishment, or embarrassment, you were initiated into the world of shame, which stimulates the desire to hide yourself and your desires. You may have felt unsafe because others were trying to control you according to their schedule or values and you experienced shame and embarrassment regarding your natural body functions if you could not meet those requirements. Negative experiences like this create a powerful message about your safety, respect and relationship with your body, framing your foundational relationship to yourself and your sexuality. This negative influence could initiate defensive and protective behaviors to avoid invasion and criticism from others.

Anything that influenced your relationship with your body and your innate acceptance of your sexuality also influences how you relate to your creativity, since your sexual energy and creative energy are the same power. Everything is in relationship with everything and there is no part of your body, mind, emotions or spirit that is separated from your divinity no matter what your beliefs are or how you feel about yourself. Separation is an illusion of the mind and has no reality base in the universal principles.

DIRECTIVES

To release yourself from these limitations, it is necessary to recognize that the illusion of separation is part of our socialization. Then you can begin to consciously change your beliefs and actions that influence your relationship with your body and others in your life.

**Learning to love you, just as you are, and
being willing to respect and have an intimate,
loving relationship with all parts of yourself
is the first step to balanced healthy living.**

Your body is a sacred temple and as you recognize this and claim the perfectly natural function each part of your body plays, you can respond in appreciation and gratitude for the living miracle of your body. Since your wholeness is innate, you can begin to feel whole again and radiantly alive, which is your natural state of being. Without a healthy appreciation for your body, you are truly disabled, no matter how brilliant your mind. You are a divine trilogy of body, mind, and emotions, surrounded by your soul. (See Illustration at the end of this section) Each part needs recognition, appreciation and movement to create balanced living.

Your relationship with your physical reality determines the values you live with in your outer world and your soul values form the foundation for your inner world through self-confidence, self-esteem and self-worth. As a child your soul values and the joy and curiosity about life motivated you. As you seek to return to your inner values, your life experiences and relationships may change dramatically. The harmony you create between your human values and your soul values underlie all the choices you make in you life. Self-love is innate no matter how you were influenced growing up.

UNIFIED FIELD

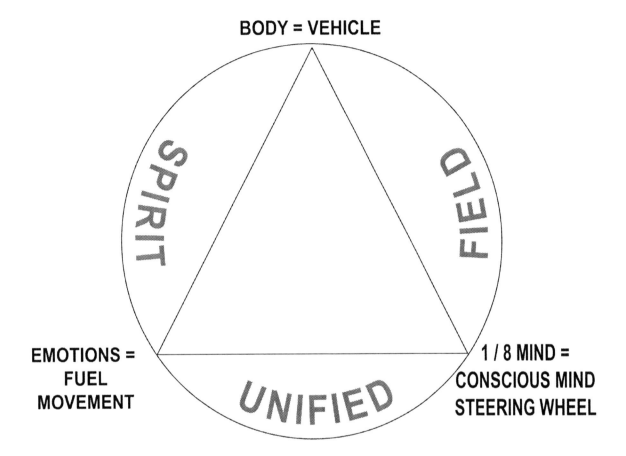

BODY = VEHICLE

SPIRIT

FIELD

EMOTIONS =
FUEL
MOVEMENT

UNIFIED

1 / 8 MIND =
CONSCIOUS MIND
STEERING WHEEL

Symbolically the circle represents spirit, the divine, universal consciousness, the infinite. Straight lines represent human existence in a three dimensional world.

This model represents that all life is created and sustained in the unified field represented through the circle. Within this circle is the triangle representing the body, conscious mind, and emotions of the human being.

Everything is energy and information. The body is the vehicle for your soul to manifest in this dimension and is a slower vibrational field, which allows you to stay in physical form and be visible to others.

The conscious mind, 1/8, is the steering wheel for your physical vehicle. Through the conscious mind you make the choices that determine your daily direction in your life. The vibrational field of the conscious mind moves faster than the body and is limited by your life conditions, experiences and beliefs.

The emotional body does not even reside within the physical structure. There are no organs or systems designed to house the emotions: emotions move through your body and provide the fuel/energy for movement. The emotions are *energy in motion,* and move at the fastest vibrational rate of any part of your humanness. Your emotions are the bridge to your soul. When you refuse to listen to your heart, the doorway to your soul, you are constricting the movement of the power of your emotional body to support you in your daily life.

FOCUS

- **Trust**

  Your heart and soul are the guiding force in your life. Your inner knowing of truth is an eternal beacon for your choices in life. Trust yourself first and everyone else in life will become trustworthy, or you will be able to discern the difference.

- **Self-respect**

  No one else has your fingerprints. No one else has your values or recognition of the quality of life you want for yourself. Listen and trust what you know from your heart's desires and wisdom.

- **Courage**

  It takes courage to be different, to be your authentic self. Your reward for having the courage to live your life according to your inner values and truth is stability and balance as your life foundation.

GUIDELINES & QUESTIONS

1. Do you love your body? List 10 qualities of your body that you love.

2. What part/parts of your body do you not love? List them.

3. What do you not love about these parts and why? How does this affect your sexuality?

4. Do you feel safe and confident in your body?

5. Do you recognize that your body is the vehicle for your soul? What does this mean to you?

6. What 3 qualities about yourself do you like the most?

7. In what ways are you dissatisfied with yourself?

8. Do you believe you can change these traits? Are you willing to?

5 to 7½ Years

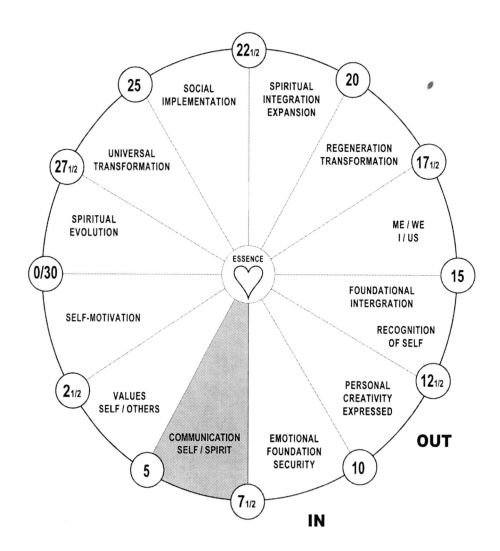

THEME

Communication
Personal
Spiritual
Self-trust

Chapter 6

Communications

POWER

Words become the tools of interaction in this cycle. At this age, your vocabulary increased and you had the ability to put more of your expression into words. The universe is full of words. You learned to use words as a primary way of relating to others. The words you heard began to define the reality you experienced and the way you learned to express yourself. Even though your vocabulary was increasing you were still very much in touch with your heart's desires and your inner reality of the timeless/formless world of dreams, visions and imagination.

The influence of language and how we are imprinted by the sounds of language were dramatically represented to me when I was in Italy visiting a family whose little girl was then 18 months old, the same age as my grandson living in the United States. Since I do not speak Italian, I could hear her sounds but was unable to recognize if they were words or just baby sounds. I asked her daddy was she making words of just sounds. He said that the majority was just sounds; he named the three or four words she was saying at that time. The inflections of her sounds were Italian because that is what she was hearing everyday in her life.

I realized that my grandson living in the U.S. was listening to English, and beginning to frame his reality through the sounds of English. If he were here in Italy, he too would be making Italian baby sounds to express himself. At this exact moment, two children of the same age were beginning to structure their reality by the sounds of the language around them and the words they would learn to use to express themselves throughout their lives, until, and if, they learn other languages. If they were exposed to several languages at this age, they would be repeating more sounds, and providing their mind with the opportunity to receive information in more than one language.

One-eighth of your mind is a conscious, linear, analyzing information field. This is the part that learns a language, communicates, spells and does math, guides you as you drive your car and cook your meals. This one-eighth is the part of your mind that is trainable. (Illustration following) The primary purpose of the conscious mind is to act as a guide and guardian for your physical body to help keep you safe and healthy: remember to drink water, eat food, rest, exercise, stay warm, cool off, etc.

Even though we are a formidable life force, we are still just packaged in a thin layer of skin; that is vulnerability. Think what would happen if every day you drove on the highway and never knew which way the traffic would be going. This would be very dangerous for your life. Simple things that we take for granted are regulated and recognized by your conscious mind to help you function safely in your human world.

In a technological, so called "civilized" society, you were trained to be heavily invested in the 1/8 reality: linear, sequential thinking. This part of your mind is similar to a computer, like a software program. Whatever programming you received from society when you were growing up, is the program you use to store information and create your reality, until you can recognize and replace the program. Using the *Wheel Of Life Cycles* is one of the ways you can consciously support yourself to create, modify, or delete your previous programming. Your 1/8 conscious mind, because it is easily programmed, is available and willing to respond to new and different ways of thinking, believing and acting if you will give yourself permission to bring in new ideas and beliefs. Be conscious of what you are putting in your mind's software because it will come back out in your life as beliefs, attitudes, behavior and actions.

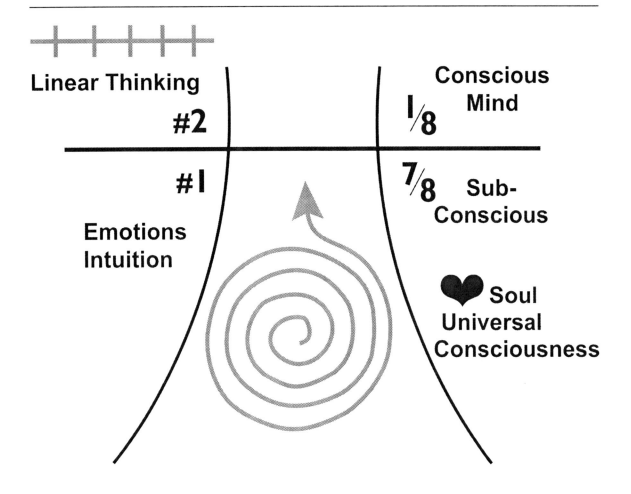

1/8 of your mind is conscious and directive and receives information in a linear sequential pattern. The conscious mind is trainable and essential for your physical well-being; its primary purpose is to keep you physically alert and safe. The conscious mind asks questions and wants to understand.

The 7/8 is your sub-conscious and is the connection to your heart and soul and universal consciousness. The 7/8 energy moves as a spiral with emotions, intuition and inner awareness. This energy is non-rational, sensory, sensual and receptive. The 7/8 receives your eternal wisdom and responds with wisdom from your heart and soul to the questions created by the 1/8, conscious mind. Life is much more balanced and stable when your 1/8 mind listens and lives from your heart'choices.

When you were born you lived in the 8/8, wholeness of your reality. You are trained through academics and life conditions to rely on the 1/8 and disregard the 7/8, which is your inner wisdom - universal power. At this time in your life you can consciously reconnect with your wholeness by reuniting with your 7/8, your heart and soul. Partnership is the key; each part of your mind is essential for your balance and both have a perfect part to play in your life.

VULNERABILITY

Through education and social conditioning you were mentally programmed to override your 7/8 reality, your heart and soul, your inner wisdom. Many of the programs you received, while growing up, were very disrespectful and discounting of your inner wisdom which receives your visions, imagination, intuition, and your universal connection to all life. Creating doubt and disassociation from your inner wisdom, influenced your sense of belonging and trusting yourself, from the inside out. That split in consciousness that got created from 2½ - 5 years of age continues to play out in your life choices.

You may have been told that what you could see, feel, and hear from your inner wisdom was not true. You may have felt you were lying or making up stories if you did not know that your inner wisdom could look and feel very differently than your outer world. Your everyday world probably provided no support for your acceptance and understanding of your intuition and your ability to see the formless/timeless world of your angels and invisible playmates. As a result, you probably began to doubt your inner wisdom, because you were not supported to validate your unseen world of personal wisdom and visions.

In the 5 to 7½ years cycle, a major split takes place between your conscious mind (1/8), and your inner wisdom, the heart and soul intelligence (7/8). If you are not supported to preserve your trust of yourself and your connection to your inner wisdom, the academic world requires your focus to be in the 1/8 conscious mind, increasing this illusion of separation between your conscious mind and your inner wisdom. This can be the beginning of diminishing your natural relationship with your abiding joy and inner wisdom that gives life to your creative expression.

Einstein said we cannot solve the problems at the same level we created them. The reality created from the 1/8 conscious mind and influencing the human condition is filled with confusion, harm, challenges, growth, change, possibilities and many other conditions we generate from our conscious mind and the choices we make. Using innate and inner wisdom of the 7/8 reality, you can go beyond the human conditions you have created and actualize the potential of your life at another level of balance and harmony using universal principles that include all life. This is what Einstein is referring to, our ability to access the unified field and use our conscious mind and inner wisdom in partnership to create a different lifestyle. Deep heart listening includes the conscious mind and the inner wisdom which are necessary in your daily life for creation to give birth to infinite potential.

DISCOVERIES

Because your mind and heart live in the same body, they are meant to function as partners, similar to the dynamics of the positive and negative currents of electricity. Without teamwork, there is only static. . .unclear thinking generates many doubts, fears and worries; feeling separated your mind and your inner wisdom cannot function as clear partners. You will feel split. Every day your inner wisdom will try and fill in this gap with your conscious mind, seeking to provide what you need to function in a balanced way in your daily life.

Inner conflict becomes a way of life when your inner wisdom and conscious mind are not on the same team, going in the same direction and listening to each other. This drastically diminishes the quality of your life and uses up huge amounts of your energy. It is natural for the conscious mind and inner wisdom to be in working partnership. As soon as you make a conscious choice to listen to your inner wisdom, that voice and awareness will become more active and increase the influence and power that is innately yours to assist your life, through grace and greater ease, which decreases stress and struggle on a daily basis.

Your ability, as a child to freely associate, to see and feel your whole reality, is your natural state of being. Your mind and heart are eternal partners always waiting for another chance to play and create together, no matter how old you are. The more influences you receive linguistically and academically during your life, the more shadowed your inner wisdom may become, unless there is a conscious effort to maintain balance with your creativity through music, movement, nature, dance, art etc.

Learning a language influences your natural state of being and alters your relationship with the universe. For example in most languages, there are many aspects of the universe that cannot be described or put into words, and yet these unspoken aspects daily influence our lives and our relationships. Your inner wisdom is always seeking to bridge this sense of separation. Music is a wonderful bridge, a common language between the heart and mind: middle C is middle C around the world and needs no translation. You are connected to all forms of life more than you consciously recognize or believe and this connection with all life, through your inner wisdom of your heart and soul is bringing you energy and information on your life path.

During this cycle in your life, through the words you share with your family, friends, teachers, neighbors, you are heavily influenced by their response to you; you are learning whether to trust yourself and your inner wisdom, or question and doubt yourself based on how they respond to you. You learn what is acceptable and safe to talk about and what is not, according to how others respond to you. As other's opinions and remarks challenge you. You may begin to question what you are seeing, hearing and feeling. This perpetuates the growing split inside you between your physical world and spiritual world. Your conscious mind, now developing as a filter, looks at your life experience and becomes confused about "who is telling the truth, them or my feelings"? This influences your own sense of self-worth, self-confidence and self-esteem. Who can you believe if the stories are different?

DIRECTIVES

When you doubt yourself and believe more in others' opinions, you feel torn and conflicted inside. This sense of separation, within you, is an illusion that feels very real. Even though the veil of unconsciousness appears, you are always part of the Divine Plan, whether you know it or not. There are no accidents in the Divine Plan. You are never "lost", which is a feeling supported only by the illusion of separation based on an outer related value system, the one that ignores inner wisdom. You may participate in a lifetime of seeking to regain the unity between your mind and inner wisdom yet you can never be separated from your soul even if you lose trust in yourself and your inner wisdom. Your soul is always calling you home, through your heart, to feel the power of your truth and your inner wisdom. Sometimes your head and heart will never feel re-united, as they were when you were a child. Sometimes it feels like it takes a lifetime to reconnect your head and heart and feel the power of unity within you again. Don' t give up! It is never too late to reunite your mind and your inner wisdom. Separation is only an illusion, experienced by the conscious mind and influenced by life's programming.

Your heart and mind are never separated. They live in the same body. The conscious mind can hear the voice of your heart and soul, and it is innate in listening to your inner wisdom. Your heart and soul remain present and powerful, waiting to be of service in your life. When you learn the language of deep heart listening and open your mind to hear your inner wisdom you can feel, once again, the partnership with your soul, this is your soul mate. The illusions of separation and being alone can be released. You are home when your conscious mind and inner wisdom work together as partners.

Remembering who you truly are is the beginning of all recovery involved in the human condition. Your conscious mind is filled with curiosity about life and can be opened to embrace the infinite possibilities in life, when given a chance to create again by reuniting with your inner wisdom.

FOCUS

- **Self- trust**

  Everything is energy and information and that connection is eternal. Everything outside of that is temporal and changing. Your inner world is valid and available to support your life consistently if you will just listen.

- **Experience**

  No matter how another perceives or describes the same experience in life, it will never look, sound or feel the same. Each individual has their window of reality. Trust your version because it is your experience, even if it is very different from another's.

- **Unity**

  Life is not "either/or" or "right or wrong" it is a continuous set of circumstances and experiences that are uniquely developed in your life. Every life experience has its perfect place in the circle of life.

GUIDELINES & QUESTIONS

1. What did you learn about yourself in this chapter?
2. Do you have a different recognition of language and words now?
3. Has your judgment or opinion of others been influenced by this information?
4. How do you feel about silence when relating to others? yourself?
5. How do you use words to get the attention you are seeking?
6. Do you have a situation in your life right now that is caused by confusion in your thinking and not listening to your heart?
7. What do you need to do to clean this up?

7½ to 10 Years

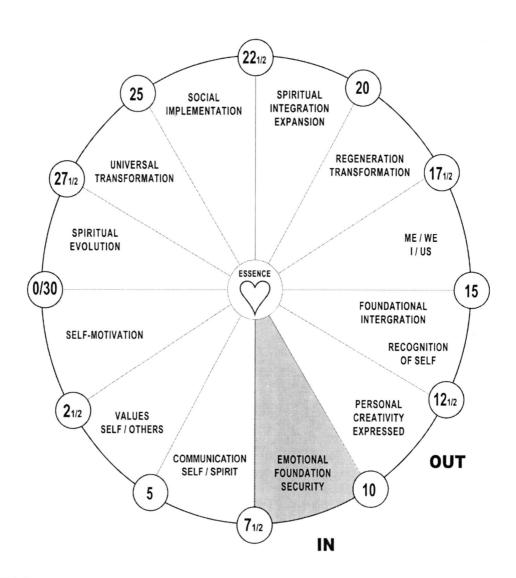

THEME

>   Home
>   Family/foundation
>   Emotional Security

Chapter 7

Emotional Foundation

POWER

Your life and experiences in this cycle deeply and profoundly influenced your sense of safety, feeling nurtured and your emotional security and foundation. This is the time for your emotional body to be stabilized and anchored in, like roots of a tree going deeper, so the tree can grow stronger and taller. Your emotional foundation was strengthened, or weakened, by what you perceived and experienced in being cared for, since birth and particularly through this age period.

This is the cycle of feeling nurtured by going deeply IN-inside, into your inner awareness, into your innermost feelings, thoughts, emotions, visions, dreams.

If you felt nurtured, loved, acknowledged and appreciated during this cycle of life it strengthens your receptivity, sensitivity, and compassion. These qualities are powerful support as you continue to grow in life and relate to others.

If you felt ignored, embarrassed, degraded, discounted, or abused-mentally, physically, emotionally or spiritually, this dramatically influences your emotional foundation and can create very reactive, defensive and aggressive or tend toward depression and despair.

From birth to 7½, you may have been challenged or trained to mistrust your own emotions, as well as your intuition. Because emotions generate movement and change in life, most people are very frightened of these feelings and try to "keep them under control". Have you ever tried to keep the ocean or the wind under control? The power of your emotions matches these elements. Just as you have learned to live with respect for nature's elements, it is important to learn to live with respect, appreciation and gratitude for the power of your emotions. Your breath and your emotions are the strongest indicators of your aliveness and both require constant movement. You can be as alive and healthy as you make up your mind to be when you are willing to think differently, behave in new ways, see with new eyes and listen to your inner wisdom, your direct line to all that is.

What would happen in your life if you committed to feeling as alive, curious and adventuresome as a child, and actually allowed yourself to develop a partnership with your emotions to motivate and enhance that aliveness?

The power of your emotional body is infinite, and it is the revolving door to your heart and soul, your inner wisdom. Even when you think you do not recognize or feel your emotions, they are registered in your neurological system as imprints. They remain available to you to be experienced and developed, or cleared, as your mind opens to greater levels of trusting yourself and becoming partners with your emotions. Depending on the experience associated with the emotions this will determine whether your unconscious response is a joyful or fearful reaction.

VULNERABILITY

Even if your caregivers did not consciously recognize that their behavior was harmful to you when you were growing up, unintentional acts of hurt or abuse that you may have experienced as a child are still equally debilitating. I truly believe that most hurtful and abusive experiences are committed through innocence and ignorance by adults simply not knowing the depth of their impact on a child's sensitivity. Through the words used, the tone of voice or attitude and behavior displayed by adults, a child's sense of safety and comfort is created or distorted.

There seems to be many acts of abuse to our children today. We may be more conscious about what constitutes abuse or it may be truly increasing, and certainly more is being revealed now than ever before.

Many times when you recognize and reveal your emotional pain from your childhood, your parents or the adult caregivers *do not even remember the incident,* yet the emotional influence on your life was deep and hurtful and remains into your adulthood. Your parents or the adults in your life may have been so stressed by their own lives that they were energetically and emotionally unavailable or disassociated from themselves and you as a child. This can create your feeling emotionally abandoned or neglected, even when they were physically present. These are the life experiences that are usually so shocking to a parent when they discover how their children feel because they were so involved in doing what they thought was "necessary" to be a good parent. In most cases, they had no idea that you felt emotionally abandoned or neglected.

As a child, what may appear to you, or have been experienced by you, as intentional abuse is spawned from the same place as unconscious abuse. When the abuser is hurt and wounded at deep levels in their early development, the limbic part of their brain maintains a primal control for survival. When their life is based on surviving, this usually does not allow the appropriate development of compassion and nurturing, mentally, physically and emotionally. In your life, you have the opportunity to be the one that breaks this pattern of abuse by awakening to the truth of who you are and making different choices in your beliefs and actions. This is a courageous and incredible gift to your ancestors and your grandchildren.

DISCOVERIES

What you perceived as damaging and painful, even when it was unintentional, still influences your sense of security, emotional foundation and safety until it is restructured. Do not doubt yourself, if the memory of your experience is different than another's perception of the same experience. As you review this cycle in your life and check out your "inner movie", see if you were carefree and joyous, sad and somber, or angry and rebellious or any other feelings. Whatever feelings you had at this time in your life will give you a clue to your emotional foundation you developed at this age, and help you discover any missing pieces that you have in your life now.

Whatever you hate, resist, resent, blame, shame, judge,
or relate to with guilt, you are chained to.

Your life and energy is never your own, nor under your direction, if you are attached to others through these feelings. Forgiveness is the key. You must forgive yourself first which allows you to begin to see and experience your world from another level of understanding and perception so forgiveness can emerge for those who you feel harmed you. You release and re-claim your life through forgiveness, never through resentment and resistance.

This release may take time to change or it may happen upon recognition. It will happen. Forgiveness frees you to be a sovereign Being and create your life from your heart and soul no matter what your life conditions have been like.

All life is energy and encoded information. Your **body** is the vehicle through which the "energy" of the soul has expression in the physical world. (see the Illustration on page 39) Your **conscious mind** is the steering wheel that guides your direction in life based on the choices you make. The conscious mind's job is to make sure your body is safe and supported in this three dimensional world; remembering what side of the street to drive on, eat food, brush your teeth, discern what is hot and cold etc. Your **emotions** are the fuel for movement. Without this power you would not be a sentient being taking action in life and demonstrating creation.

When emotions get relegated to a polarized value system that says, "this feeling is good, or this feeling is bad," you learn to deny the power of the emotions as a direct expression from your soul experienced in your body as a power for motivation and change.

Instead of registering emotions and labeling them right or wrong, give yourself the opportunity to just feel the emotion/s, register the *quantity* of this power rather than *qualify* this power (good/bad, right/wrong etc), then you can have an intimate relationship with your emotions as a divine part of yourself, rather than some intrusive energy that you have to control, suppress or deny. When you accept your emotions as a healthy, natural part of your life you can accept this power, feel safer with your emotions and take conscious responsibility for directing your behavior. Emotions that are allowed to flow and move do not kill people. Behavior and reactions in life kill people. Behavior that is not managed, and generated from suppressed emotions, can be detrimental inside - to your immune system, and outside - in all your relationships and life circumstances.

As an Energy Being, you are inter-connected with all life and need to be as conscious of your "emotional pollution" as you are of air and water pollution. You emotionally pollute your body and your relationships when you refuse or deny responsibility for your feelings, by blaming someone else for how you feel. No one can *make you* feel anything. Your emotions are completely personal and live and move through your body and belong only to you. Your reaction or response to someone's behavior is very personal and many times not even associated with the current experience, but triggered from neurological responses from your early childhood imprints.

You keep your emotional field "clean" by feeling your feelings and being responsible for the way you direct your power. Your feelings belong to you, a gift of universal power and *you are not your feelings*. Your feelings/emotions are divine energy designed to move through your body in a similar manner as your blood moving through your circulatory system, keeping everything alive and clean. Movement is life. Everything has movement and purpose in life. Emotions are a vital part of your life, like blood is a vital part of the circulatory system. Emotions generate powerful movement in your physical world by providing the energy and motivation to create. It is essential that you unite with your emotions as a divine part of your human life and consciously develop appropriate ways to use and direct this power for the highest good of all life.

What you can feel you can heal.

What you can recognize you can direct.

There are no enemies inside of you. All parts of you come from the same source of creation and are manifestations of love. Any part of you, programmed by your life experiences, that feels conflicted and at war within you, can be changed to be more congruent with your heart and soul's blueprint. Changing your belief system is the gateway to changing your behavior, attitudes and life experiences. Your conscious mind is always receptive to new programming. Become conscious of what you are thinking so you can create the life that you desire.

DIRECTIVES

Review your "life movie" from 7½ - 10 years old into the present time and see how your emotional foundation, created during this cycle, has been an influence in every phase of your life. Unrecognized feelings are similar to a low-grade fever in the body, they are always influencing your health and wellness and seemingly from an unknown cause. When you review your life, be a compassionate observer and recognize what a good job you have done to get yourself to this moment of life with crucial pieces of your emotional foundation unrecognized, weakened or missing. You might also discover that these years have generated some unrecognized strength as well. Emotional challenges, many times, provide blessings in your life later on that seemed impossible as you were going through them as a child.

Letting go of labeling your feelings and beginning to recognize them as a quantity of divine power, you can then determine by the "amount of emotion" whether you have the power and support for a small movement in life or a large movement in life. Labeling your emotions for your mental satisfaction and the comfort of identification minimizes the power by whatever label you use because it then becomes captured in your mind's description and reaction to what that label means, individually and collectively. Emotions are fuel for movement. If your whole body feels full with your emotions, this indicates you have a lot of power/fuel so you can move your life in a process that may be on going for a while. This emotional power will sustain you as long as you need it. If you have a smaller amount of emotion in your body, your movement with the condition at hand is probably fairly simple or short term. In order to build a strong emotional foundation, which increases your confidence and sense of security, you must develop a trusting relationship with your own emotions. Fearing your own emotional power is a no win situation for you.

Emotions are a natural power activated in the moment as a present time experience. Your mind may attach a memory to the emotion and recall a time when you felt like this before and translate that memory into the present experience, or project into the future, based on the fear of the past. (see the Illustration at the end of this section) The empty spaces you have from your childhood can be consciously filled today by using the emotional power of your present experiences and not allowing your mind to disassociate from the experience by going into the past or the future. If you allow your mind to leave the moment you are in, you continue to have your emotional responses associated with yesterday's feelings or tomorrow's fears, rather than experiencing a different outcome based on what is actually happening today.

If your mind is dictating the experience from memory of the past or fear of the future instead of being present with the current experience, you will keep getting the same results, whether today's conditions have changed or not. Continuing to react from yesterday's emotions or tomorrow's fears creates a mind loop that you can avoid by staying present emotionally, to the fullness of your ability, in each moment's experience.

Your experiences and beliefs influence your emotional foundation. Changing your beliefs can begin at any moment when you decide to think and feel differently about yourself and your life experiences. (Erroneous Zones by Wayne Dyer is a good book about this topic). The conscious mind is easily programmed and innately only wants to serve your physical safety, so when you begin to think differently, your emotions have an opportunity to move in new ways and your life will begin to look and feel differently, whether anything outside of you changes or not. A peaceful world is an inside job: this is our personal responsibility and is available to every one of us now.

When you establish an intimate, working relationship with your emotions, you become an active co-creator with your inner wisdom. In this partnership you can be a conscious participant directing some of the most powerful energies you can access as a human being. When you feel empowered, you can come to a place of forgiveness for those who you experienced or perceived as hurting you. When you establish a different relationship with your personal emotions, all other relating experiences are influenced by this change and you will feel the sense of fulfillment that occurs when you take charge of directing your emotional power.

Your conscious mind is the only part of you that can leave the Present experience. Where your feet are is where your heart and body are. Your mind can go wandering into the Past and stress about, "If only I had or had not done…" or project into the Future and fill it with fear, doubt and worry about "What if…" When you learn to manage your thinking and keep it in the moment you are in, then your emotions reflect the Present experience. If your mind identifies the emotion of the moment and attaches to a memory in the Past, then today's experience will be clouded over by the memory of this Past experience, and you will miss the actual experience of this Present moment. This is how you use your mind to keep bringing your past emotional experiences into your Present life. Emotions are a Present time experience. They happen in the moment you are living in now. Your mind is what makes the connection to the Past or projects into the future.

Past	Present	Future
If Only...	1/8 Cons Mind	What If...
	Feet	

FOCUS

- **Vulnerability**

  This is your ability to be open and present with your own emotions and any feelings without denial, disassociating, deflecting or projecting. This guarantees you will be fully present in this moment of your life.

- **Receptivity**

  The power of your mind and heart to be available to receive guidance in partnership with your intuition which is essential for balanced stress free living.

- **Openness**

  When you are open, your innocence and curiosity about life are active and available to create life in new adventuresome ways. This supports spontaneity in your life.

GUIDELINES & QUESTIONS

1. How do you feel right now?

2. Is this how you want to feel? If not, change your focus and change your feelings.

3. Are you willing to take responsibility for your life through taking ownership of your emotional power?

4. What is the worst thing that could happen to you as a result of taking ownership of your emotional power?

5. What is the best thing that could happen to you as a result of taking ownership of your emotional power?

6. Now what do you want to create with this owned power?

.

10 to 12½ Years

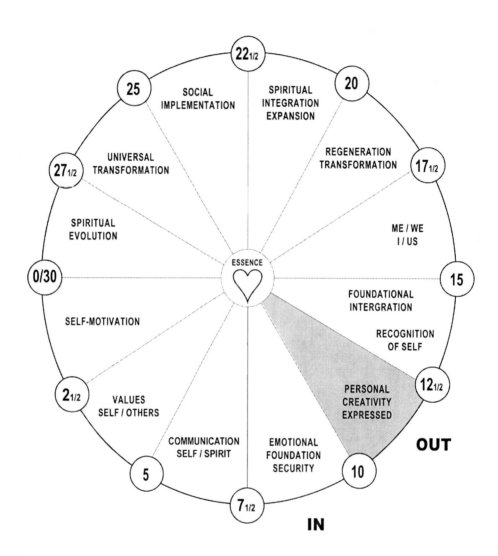

THEME

  Expression
  Creativity
  Aliveness

Chapter 8

Personal Creativity

POWER

What part of you has been "on hold" and is waiting to be expressed? What were your inner dreams and visions when you were 10 - 12½? Are you living any of them now? What happened to interfere with these dreams becoming your reality? The power of this cycle is in your potential to create your heart's desires and share them with others.

Now is the time for your inner desires to come OUT. During this cycle your interests begin to widen according to your confidence and you want to "try" many different activities, sports, music, dance, and organizations exploring the varied avenues of creativity that you are opening to. Since there are no particular labels or social categories for you to fit into at this age, seeking your creative expression is part of your identity and these years are really an important gateway to your finding your own personal power for your inner creative expression. If you don't fit the social norms and don't feel comfortable with your own routines, emotions or behaviors, your life is ripe for change, ready to be created anew. This is an important time in your life. Your passion and creativity are seeking expression, a way out, to demonstrate your creativity. Your power is unlimited potential with infinite possibilities. Important as this is, many times it is a very uncomfortable, vulnerable, hurtful time in your life if you do not feel you have the safety, comfort, and guidance you so desperately want in order to feel safe so you could "just go for it".

When you consciously open these doors again to your inner creative expression, something magical happens in your ordinary daily life - it takes on new meaning, new purpose, new joy, and new hope. Then you know you are truly accessing your own hidden or buried treasure chest of talents and the abilities that you agreed, as a soul, to share with the world. Even when you discover these hidden talents, you may still feel fearful, insecure, shy, or lack self-confidence to demonstrate them. These are natural feelings at any age when you discover a way for you to creatively express yourself, especially if it is a new venture. Have the courage to take that first step and continue until you gain your sense of confidence with your creativity. Baby steps are good. . . giant leaps are sometimes fun and not necessary to make the changes that you desire. These feelings are a clue to let you know you are tapping on the door of your creative potential that may have been waiting to blossom since this cycle from 10 to 12½ years.

VULNERABILITY

These two years are like a big buffet of creativity and you may or may not be able to determine which avenue best suits your creative expression. You may end up with "many avenues" for you to use as your expression in the world; you don't have to have "one avenue", you may have many. Without some avenue this will leave a void in your life because your personal creativity is a divine gift that brings you great joy and is part of your purpose for being on this planet. If your creativity door does not open for your heart's desire, so you can share it with others, a part of you will feel unfilled throughout your life until you open that door. Creativity is infinite. . . .you can express it at any time that you decide you want to. Now is a great time!!

This cycle was such an amazing time in your growing up years. At this age, your body seemed to grow in spurts so you may have felt clumsy and uncoordinated, your baby teeth were still falling out so chances are you didn't like the way you looked, and your energy and emotions were like a roller coaster. One day you wanted to still be a child, the next day you wanted to be "grown up", and yet you were not sure how to do either. Your creativity was high and wanting to come out in every way possible, rarely making any sense or having any consistency. Your creativity had hit a new level of intensity, activated by the pre-puberty or puberty power, and you were trying to adjust to this inner explosion. There was so much going on inside of you at this time that your outer world and reality did not appear or feel the same to you. Your behavior may have been very reactive or hidden on practically every level and occasion, which was confusing to you as well as everyone else.

In our society there is not even a term used for this age. You were not an infant or a toddler. Even though you felt like a child many times yet you did not want to be treated like one most of the time. You were not a teen, sometimes called a pre-teen, so there was really no clear" label" for you at this age. Growing up in a society that labels and categorizes everything, without a "label", no one knew what to do with you, or how you fit in, and you were living in the middle of all these feelings, just trying to figure out what to do with yourself. Remember those feelings? If you didn't have a structure or system to fit into and know the rules that defined getting approval and recognition, how could you feel safe and get attention in a healthy way? You may remember many experiences where you felt embarrassed or misrepresented by others because they didn't know what to do with you either, or how to relate to you, and yet everyone was doing the best they knew how. Everyone was uncomfortable. The emerging process is natural and not necessarily comfortable or easy. The rewards for going through this cycle and trying many avenues of expression and experience are invaluable as you continue your life cycles.

DISCOVERIES

During this cycle, you need to have exposure to a variety of methods and opportunities to express your own ideas, talents, skills, abilities and check out your dreams to see if you really have interest in pursuing any of them. At this age, you may have found some creative avenues of expression and stuck with them, or you may have tried many avenues until something really clicked for you. Consistency in expressing your creativity was probably not what was happening at this age, change was the norm. Your parents may have felt that you were being irresponsible because you did not "pick something to do" and stick with it.

You can learn a lot about your level of confidence and willingness to expose your creative abilities in your life now, based on reviewing the responses and reactions of your peers, siblings, family and community during this cycle. At this age, your peers began to become the "god" in your life. What was most important was to be recognized by your peers and have their approval. If you expressed yourself and the response that came back from your peers felt threatening, unkind or disapproving, no matter how strong your passion to express, chances are you immediately diluted it, suppressed it or ignored it. Negating yourself for any reason is a big and long-term price to pay for approval. When you recognize this, you can reclaim and activate your creativity at any time in your life by becoming self-referenced, listening once again to your inner wisdom. What do you REALLY want to do regardless of others response?

If your creativity feels unfamiliar or unknown to you, then chances are you did not recognize or develop a conscious relationship with this aspect of yourself as a youth. Whatever you can recognize you can direct and give expression to, so now may be the time. When you begin to consciously relate with your inner creative self, all kinds of feelings may come up and they are a natural part of the process. Feel the feelings and keep moving. Remember your emotions are the fuel for movement in your life. No matter what your emotions are, they are the energy and support for you to move forward in your life and create the life that you desire.

When you begin to recognize your talents and gifts, you will feel more connected to your inner wisdom and creativity than you ever dreamed possible and you can make your contribution in life motivated by your passions. You are a co-creator with a deep heart's desire to be seen, heard and recognized. You make a difference in life living and expressing your gifts and talents, even if you do not consciously recognize this.

DIRECTIVES

Review your childhood and these years particularly from 10 to 12½ and allow yourself to remember what your dreams and visions were at that age. Now is the time to let those dreams become a reality. Whatever creativity you want to express allow yourself to explore as many options as you desire until you find some creative expressions that provide a way for your inner passion to have a powerful demonstration in your life. Creativity released blesses the whole world. This journey of developing a relationship with your creative self is like a safari, going into unknown territory, and it is good to have a guide until you gain confidence to go on your own. Enroll in classes, join groups of like-minded people, take tours with others, check on the Internet, hire a coach. . . whatever will increase your exposure to other ways to live and express.

In the economic world, with productivity and consumer based values, creativity has had little or no value. Yet through out the ages, what is remembered and cherished in all civilizations is spawned from creativity that is not economically based. The creators are usually not recognized or appreciated until they are dead. So if you use the economic value system to evaluate your hearts desires, you will never understand nor prioritize creativity in your life. You may want to re-evaluate and revise your value system so that your heart and soul are the driving force for your life, not economics or approval from others. It is essential for your wellness and balance in life to be "seen, heard and recognized". In order to achieve this, you must *see, hear and recognize yourself*, who you really are. When your life is self-referenced you will not have the same value system nor be motivated by the same demands of an outer defined valued system; one that says in order for you to be important you "have to do life this way", according to others values. When you claim your value in life, life has a whole different value system that you can recognize and relate to that provides an expanded level of freedom in your personal life.

FOCUS

- **Listen**

  Have the courage to hear your deep heart's longing. This is where your passion and power reside for creating.

- **Trust**

  Trust your heart. Trust your desire. Trust your curiosity and spontaneity. Then take action on these truths.

- **Enjoy**

  Joy is the voice of the soul in your ordinary daily life. If you are not enjoying your life or in joy about life, your soul does not have a voice. Your creativity is an expression for the joy of your soul.

GUIDELINES & QUESTIONS

1. What is your heart longing to do?

2. What fears are keeping you from doing this?

3. What are the benefits to your life if you express your heart's desires?

4. What is the price you pay if you do not?

5. Everyday for two weeks list five things you recognize and appreciate about yourself.

6. If you could not fail, what would you do to express your creativity?

12½ to 15 Years

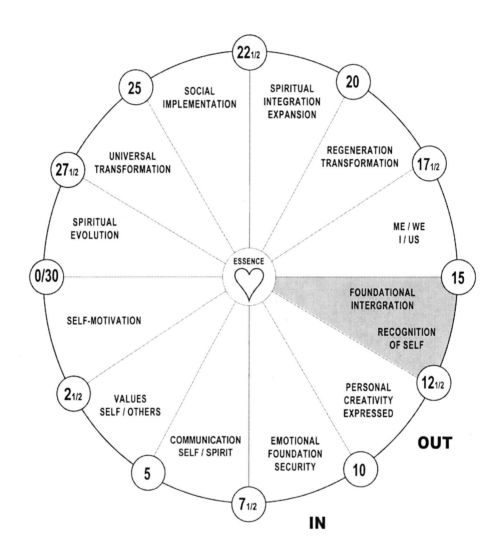

THEME

    Integration
    Stabilizing
    Strengthening

Chapter 9

Integration

POWER

This cycle integrates and weaves all of your life experiences together from birth to fifteen years of age. You are being exposed and becoming familiar with your own power, including your sexual energy. The relationship you establish with your personal power and how it is being used in your daily life creates your foundation emotionally, mentally, physically, and spiritually for the next 15 years. Your life experiences up to this point are the building blocks for your future. Your soul is the true guide in your life and is initiating integration in this cycle for your foundation to be as strong as possible based on your experiences from birth which have influenced your confidence and self-worth. This is a major Rite of Passage into adulthood. Whether society has created the initiations or not, life does. If we consciously created Rites of Passage this gateway to adulthood could be clearer and stronger, reducing your confusion about managing and directing your daily choices in life. Trial and error is the Rite of Passage when a society does not consciously create its own; you are forced to meet your next steps in life using all of this power in the best way you knew how.

At this age you may have felt quite clear about your life purpose or you could have felt clueless. Looking at your life process and using the skills and abilities you had acquired assisted you to make the best choices for your life in that moment; greatly enhancing your future, even if you felt unclear about where you were going and what you were going to be doing. The power of living in the now moment is to see your life and choices through the eyes of compassion and respect for your courage and clarity in the moment you were making those choices. Of course, you can look back now, with additional experience and exposure and critique that moment and create many more options. If these choices would have been available to you then, you might have considered them as options. When you use any age or any condition in your life as a reference for your movement in life, you want to forgive yourself, accept your choices, appreciate your current wisdom and acknowledge what you chose to do worked, you are still alive and breathing in this moment. In this moment you are the sum total of all of your life experiences and thus can begin a new life, through new choices at any given moment, regardless of age.

VULNERABILITY

You made tremendous transitions in this cycle. You were finishing elementary school, going through intermediate school and preparing to enter high school. All at once, inside and out, your life went into hyper-drive, your emotions escalated, your energy went through many highs and lows, your beliefs and attitudes changed, and the whole world may have seemed out of balance much of the time, according to your changing reality. Insecurity may have been a constant companion during those days, even when you were happy, life still was a bit wobbly inside because so much energy was shifting and moving causing everything to feel so unfamiliar. Everything that was secure or familiar before was now rapidly transforming and sometimes you could not adjust as fast as the changes were taking place. You may have felt displaced in your own life, even with those you loved and that you knew loved you. Relating with yourself and others was challenging during this time, since you were creating a new foundation to use for the next fifteen-years of your life. Life was under construction and didn't always go as planned and many changes did not add to your sense of self-confidence or self esteem, especially if the changes created any kind of conflict inside of you or with others.

DISCOVERIES

One thing you knew was that the outer world sure didn't fit with your inner world. Your reality could have felt split since you did not consciously know that you are consistently guided by your soul, living with a soul purpose and not just a personality seeking recognition. Transformation from a personality to a soul goes on unconsciously and usually causes stress in your life because you are not recognized or taught to rely on your inner wisdom, and yet your heart knows there is more to life than you believe or can recognize right now.

This is one of the most challenging times for adult/youth interrelationships, because the familiar patterns for relating are completely disrupted by the radical changes and everyone in the family has to make drastic shifts in behavior and attitude just to have a simple conversation; no one knows how to relate to each other any more, and in most cases, what was known was not talked about. When the children become young adults the family dynamics and patterns must change to accommodate the increased responsibility and freedom that is necessary at this age. These children/young adults are preparing to go into the world of choice and confusion generated by human behavior and they need to be as strong as possible to maintain their balance, so they begin to practice this independence at home, where it hopefully is a safe, caring environment.

Everyone in the family could feel emotionally vulnerable in such powerful and intense times. Great opportunities for growth, compassion, and acceptance of each other are available every day in many ways as the family unit expands to prepare for your becoming a young adult. The generational patterning is truly revealed and challenged by the fire of the sexual/creative energy coming into your young body with such force that you are destined to change, no matter what your beliefs are. This is reflected in the words of Kahlil Gibran in The Prophet on Children:

You may house their bodies but not their souls,

for their souls dwell in the house of tomorrow,

which you cannot visit, not even in your dreams.

Without this powerful time coming into each generation, we would continue to re-create the past. The "spark of life" is designed to challenge the generational patterning to promote greater possibilities for changing the future. Even though this cycle can be one of the most challenging for adults and children, when you review this from your soul purpose you can recognize the importance in your life, to respond and recognize how your sexuality/creativity influenced change for you, your family and friends. This is such a good example of the amount of emotion you experience as an individual when the changes necessary are so significant in your life. When you make big changes you need a lot of courage and emotional power to make it possible to takes the necessary steps of action.

The main way sexuality is represented in America is as a marketing tool. As a young person, you may have had no real understanding of the creative power you were accessing at this time in your life, or that this creative power and your sexuality are the same energy. You probably did not know that as your hormones changed and the power to physically create life awakened in your body, your chakras were also activated. When these spiritual energy centers in your body, the chakras, are awakened, your access and use of the universal power, the source of all creation, increases dramatically. This is the power field that you were trying to integrate at this time in your life, without a handbook and many times with no healthy role models. This is an enormous challenge. This experience is kind of like giving the keys for a car to a 10-year-old, with no instructions and expecting them to know how to drive safely and not injure themselves or anyone else; not very realistic and very dangerous for everyone. Not knowing what to do with a lot of new energy can be exciting if you are confident and adventuresome or it can feel frightening and sometimes overwhelming if you feel unsure and out of control.

DIRECTIVES

You may recognize how extreme some of your choices seemed, during this cycle. It is essential to review this time with a benevolent heart, as an observer, and know that the more extreme your choices and behaviors were at this time, the more you were trying to manage your life, feeling unsafe and undirected with all this new energy. At the time you really did make the very best choices you knew how to make, no matter how extreme or disruptive the choices may have been to you or others. Release all judgments on yourself. Forgive yourself and re-unite with your soul by being loving, appreciative and compassionate with yourself now. This is essential for your physical, mental, and emotional balance throughout your life. Forgiveness is the key, you first.

This is an article from a teenager written to Dear Abby, a newspaper columnist that answers questions sent in to her. This provides some insight from the teenager's world.

Dear Abby:

When I was 12 years old, my mother cut an article out of your column and gave it to me. Seven years later, it's still up on my wall, though yellowed and worn from the many times I've touched it and reread it. Will you please reprint it so another "ungrateful" teenager, and perhaps his/her mother can see it before the child is grown and gone:

Dear Abby:

So many adults keep asking us "ungrateful" teenagers what we want. I finally have an answer that I think says it all:

- *I want time to be alone; alone with my thoughts*
- *I want to be accepted for what I am.*

- *I want to be loved by those who brought me into the world.*

- *I want a home that is rich in honesty, sharing and caring.*

- *I want to be heard: I just might have something that you need to hear.*

- *I want to know more about myself, my sexuality, my desires, and my goals.*

- *I want to know God and worship him in my own way.*

- *I want to live my life one day at a time; for only then will I know its fullness*

- *And as I would live my life for me, so would I have you live your life for you.*

A Teenager

FOCUS

- **Self- recognition**

Now, more than ever in your first 15 years of life, pay attention to who you are, how you feel, what do you want in life and accept what you discover.

- **Self- acceptance**

It is important to accept your uniqueness and begin to have confidence in yourself to live and think differently than others and still have friends.

- **Appreciation**

Allow yourself to recognize your inner wisdom, just as you are, and begin to appreciate the individualized qualities that make you unique and gifted. Appreciation is the reward of self-acceptance.

GUIDELINES & QUESTIONS

1. What is your greatest regret from this cycle in your life?

2. What is your greatest joy from this cycle in your life?

3. What do you want to change and claim in your life right now? You can fill in the blanks of your life during this cycle by reviewing your life with compassion and forgiveness.

4. Who was your mentor or safest adult in your life during this cycle?

5. Do they know how important they were in those years of your growing up?

6. Write them a letter of appreciation and mail it to them if you can, if not, burn it the same day written. Spirit will find their heart and deliver your appreciation and love.

15 to 17½ Years

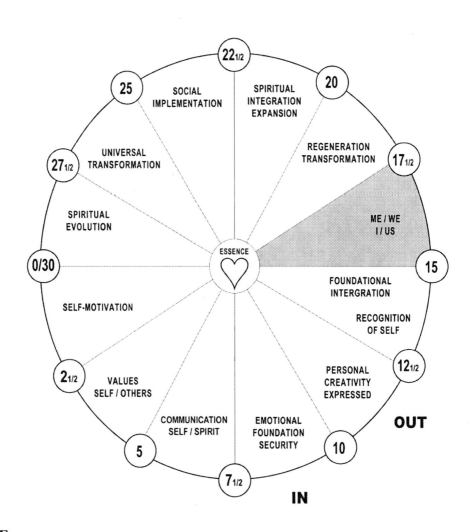

THEME

    Relating
    One on one
        Business
        Friendship
        Personal Partnerships

Chapter 10

Personal Relating

POWER

The power of this cycle is to learn how you are motivated to get the attention you desire to have your needs met while relating to another, who wants attention and to have their needs met also. Loving through cooperation, sensitivity and respect is the ultimate in relating. When you know what motivates you in seeking attention to love and be loved, the quality of your relationships will either improve or they may become less interesting to you and you might clear out relationships that are not healthy or balanced for you.

The first 15 years of your life you are building your foundation based on your experiences, consciously or unconsciously, that are molding your belief systems, your attitudes and influencing your behavior and choices. Now you begin the second 15 years in which you will use your foundational influences from birth through 15 years old to build your future upon until you are 30.

Recognizing and updating your attention and motivation pattern is one of the most rewarding things you can do for yourself. Attention is a primal need and it is your opportunity, as a young adult, to begin to take more responsibility for relating to others, especially those outside the family. As you develop more and more relationships notice what is motivating you in these relationships, what do you want or expect in these relationships? Is that what is happening or are you disappointed more often than satisfied? Getting clear on the patterns that you create in relating helps you identify your need for attention and why you make the choices that you do. Learning this at this age of young adulthood can give you years of strength and confidence in relating. Knowing your own motivations for getting attention allows you to create healthy choices and supports you to be in relationship without being motivated by blame and judgment and feeling like a victim or being in resentment towards your partner.

VULNERABILITY

The motivation model created from birth to 2½ years old, strongly influences your life, especially in this cycle from 15–17½ when you begin to develop more personal relationships and are required to relate differently than you have within your family.

If you learned as a baby, in order to get attention, you had to *make a lot of noise*, then you are imprinted with that message and will continue to sophisticate that pattern and feel compelled to *make a lot of noise* to get attention from others today. Maybe your patterning was to get sick, be quiet, cling, distance yourself or any combination of these methods. Whatever way you developed getting attention so your needs could be met is still the method you are using today in relating unless you have become conscious of these imprints and neurologically, emotionally or mentally re-directed them. These motivational patterns are very primal and not conscious since they were developed very early in your life.

If the way you seek attention is an unknown factor for you, this can create confusion because your behavior may not always have matched with what you thought you wanted, and therefore cannot bring you the desired attention and fulfillment. Relating is challenging, because each person may be unclear on what motivates their behaviors and attitudes with each other. This forces the true desires to be sublimated and you are always trying to fulfill something that you are unconscious of; always seeking to deepen your experiences on how to relate to another and still get your needs met. This may be the most precision act of balance that we all participate in as humans, conscious relating without feeling compromised. It is our nature as humans and it is an innate desire for us to "belong". We are a group species. We want to feel a part of our "human family".

At this age, your world is your peers and your relationships with them. Relating in this stage of your life is very intense. You are barely used to your expanded sexual energy challenging you emotionally, and now you are trying to find a way of relating to others while discovering more of who you are in the process. Since life does not provide a relationship handbook and instructions, you are on your own, with very few inspiring role models in partnership. As a result, you will do the best that you can in the moment and continuously learn as you go through the major classroom of life – relating.

This is a tender time in your life. You are exposing your feelings and desires in the clearest ways you know how and the responses from others are very influential in shaping your confidence and willingness to be open and vulnerable in relating to others.

DISCOVERIES

This is the time when the gateway to your heart opens to a new level of loving yourself and others. This is one of the reasons a "first love" is so influential in your life. Life experiences that are gateways to your expansion are deeply significant and usually remain as peak times of experience throughout your life.

At this age you are beginning to gain some personal identity in relating, and transcending some of your family/social patterning that influences the way you receive attention. It is important to register "gateway experiences", such as a first love, and not expect future relationship to feel the same way. Treasure these moments as one of a kind and know that you can revisit these precious moments at any time since love is eternal. By loving the experience you allow yourself to grow beyond "first love" and continue to expand your heart and love potential throughout your life.

Since your emotions are directly related to your heart and soul expressions, when you have life experiences that open your heart to another level of loving the feelings associated with this are usually never repeated in your lifetime. If you use a "first love" experience as a model for future relating, you will always be disappointed. You will continue throughout your lifetime to experience other heart openings that will allow you to love more deeply and feel a stronger connection with yourself, others and all life and yet each experience is unique unto its own expression.

DIRECTIVES

If you are reviewing this cycle in your life, do so with a lot of compassion for the unknown and your vulnerability in this stage of development. You always made the best choices you knew how based on the experiences you had. This cycle is one of the biggest and calls you, with minimum experience, into an expanded state of relating that is unfamiliar to you.

In indigenous tribes, gateway situations are called Rites of Passage and signal major life changes. The experiences that you determine as life changing and that fall into this category are beneficial for you to review. When you begin to consciously recognize them you can see how they opened the doorway of your heart and mind to receive life at new levels. Reviewing these events from a different perspective you can feel clearer and less confused or victimized, reclaiming more of your personal power and self-confidence.

Even though the western culture does not consciously create Rites of Passage, you can recognize the Wheel of Life Cycles as a series of Rites of Passage. As you move through each cycle, you can feel much more accomplished if you recognize how many you have been through and what lessons you have learned; what were the challenges and benefits of each particular gateway.

The common denominator of life is **relating**. All of your life you will be practicing relating every day in every thing you do, with plants, animals, people, conditions, your body, ideas, the earth – with all forms of life. Relating is not a destination, it is a journey of the heart and soul. Relating is the never-ending story of new things to learn with every person you meet and relate to and in every situation offered in life on a daily basis. Change is the foundation of life, and relating is the stage we all stand on as we practice our part and share our life with others.

FOCUS

- **Balance**

  You must have balance in your own life experience before you can ever have any balanced relationships in your life. Relating starts inside and moves out into the world.

- **Trust**

  Trust is an inside issue. You must first know that you can trust yourself, your heart and your soul to support your well-being in life, before you can ever practice trusting anyone else.

- **Respect**

  No matter what kind of relationship you are in with another person they are their own person and deserve to be respected and treated with loving-kindness. You do not know what is best for another person in your life. Your job is to focus on what is best for you and support another to do the same.

GUIDELINES & QUESTIONS

1. What Rites of Passage did you go through during this cycle of your life?
2. How did this Rite of Passage influence your life?
3. If you did this Rite of Passage again, how would you create it?
4. List the strengths you recognize you had during this cycle in relating with others.
5. List the areas of vulnerability in relating to others at this age.
6. Appreciate 6 things you have learned about relating since you were in this cycle.

17½ to 20 Years

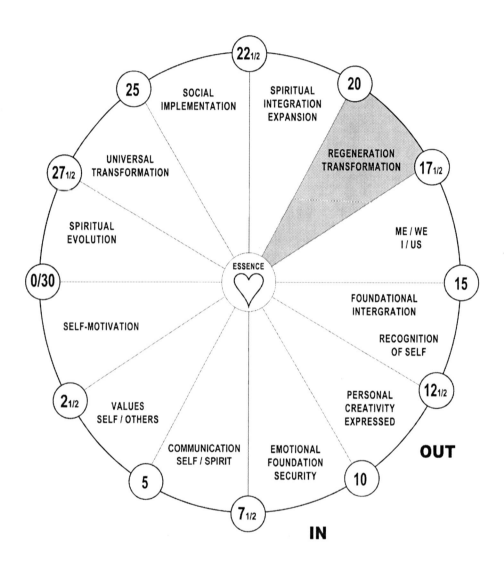

THEME

Self- empowerment
Emerging power
Personal and collective power

Chapter 11

Transformation

POWER

Green light means GO!!!!! This is the power and energy of this cycle. Every part of you – mentally, physically, emotionally, and spiritually is ready to create, to transform yourself and the world through a strong sense of your potential to influence change in the world.

Your world and the structures you live with in school and at home are expanding and you get a sample of what life could be like as an adult: doing your own thing, making your own decisions and glimpsing the bigger world of life, realizing *everything* is possible.

Power needs and demands structure. This is a time for determining how you want to focus and direct your ideas, creativity, sexuality, money, and soul purpose in life. Your inner wisdom is your innate guide throughout your life to guide and direct your conscious mind in partnership with your heart, if you are willing to listen.

VULNERABILITY

If you grew up in a home situation that felt suppressive to you, you could feel really excited about experiencing your life with all the possibilities available in this cycle including your freedom to choose how you want to live. If you lack confidence in yourself, you could feel really challenged and fearful about all this power and possibilities. This cycle plays off of your values and the level of self-esteem and confidence that you acquired or learned from 2½ to 5 years old. The way you experienced yourself and however you felt valued at this young age directly influences your sense of excitement or fear once you reach this cycle of 17½ to 20 years old.

Self-esteem and self-confidence are very personal experiences. Even for those raised in the same family, the same experiences will have a different impact on each family member. We truly do not know what makes the difference that one individual will survive extreme life conditions and come out strengthened and empowered and use the conditions in a positive way in their life. Yet another individual can go through the same conditions and be traumatized, never fully recovering their personal identity or their strength to live in a quality way.

In developing a personal relationship with your vulnerability, you create the opportunity to live and grow through this rite of passage and personally step into your power. Many people have learned to avoid their vulnerability, considering it a weakness or too overwhelming. Avoiding your vulnerability can create a crisis in your life that will force you into a vulnerable position, so you will still be required to access your vulnerability to give birth and life to your power, consciously or unconsciously.

You have choice, you can change by listening and meeting the moment when it is presented in your life or you can resist and allow a crisis to direct you to your next experience. Either way, you are destined to grow through your vulnerability into your power.

DISCOVERIES

Resiliency seems to be a key factor: the ability to meet life conditions and "bend" with the change, be flexible and adapt in order to survive. Like the trees along the coast line that have adapted to the winds off the ocean, or the trees at high altitudes that do not grow very full or tall, and still live under amazingly challenging conditions, life is a constant state of adapting and adjusting, from the inside out.

Because life is so precious and powerful, many unknown forces exist within all living things to support it. Modern science has had an amazing and humbling discovery that ninety-nine per cent of all existence is not only invisible to our senses and instruments, but without mass and structure. When life is threatened, these forces are called forth and provide whatever is necessary to meet the moment of challenge and carry us through. This life force is the element that is demonstrated in resiliency. You are more powerful than you imagine and more resilient than you experience until the challenges of life call forth these essential forces that continue to sustain your life, our planet and all the species.

Resiliency is the key for handling the transformation of power in this cycle of 17½ to 20 years old. It reminds me of how few coconut trees went down during Hurricane Iniki on September 11, 1992 on Kau'ai, Hawai'i when the winds raged from 167 mph – 227 mph. The coconut tree withstood these winds, even with a very shallow root system, because they bend and move with the wind. When we can bend and move with change, we have a far greater chance of surviving and maintaining our balance on every level of life.

Power and resiliency are natural qualities during this cycle; you haven't been in this world a long time so your experiences and potential are just being tapped by life. You can be deeply enrolled in life and your own potential in this cycle of life, which is powered by a high passion for transformation: you have innate courage to risk many changes and seek adventure in order to expand your life experience.

The power of your creative life force and your sexual energy are very strong and can be clearly focused to support your creativity, if you chose to do so. Your sexual energy and your creativity are two expressions of the same energy. Your relationship with your sexuality and your self- esteem are based on your experiences from 2½ to 5 years old. At that age your self-confidence was influenced by how you were treated, respected and valued by others, mentally, physically and emotionally.

DIRECTIVES

This cycle from 17½ - 20 deals with many of the issues of life – power, sex, money, and greed – all influencing the collective consciousness. As you became more conscious about your personal values and the issues that are influencing "all of us", you can take greater responsibility for your personal choices that influence the use of power, sex and money in your life. Collective means "all of us", so when you make choices that increase the quality of your own life, you make a powerful contribution to changing the collective consciousness for "all of us". The primary way the collective consciousness changes is from the inside out, each individual choice influences the collective consciousness. You make a difference: your choices in your life influence you and the future of our children.

The essential aspect in this cycle is to FEEL life; listen to what you personally feel, take responsibility and make choices based on your feelings, which contributes to the transformation of the use or misuse of power. Your values and choices influence the quality of your life and impact everyone and everything in life. Interconnectedness is a law of physics not just an idea.

We are 5½ - 6 billion people on one planet. We are in this together as a global family. Otherwise, why don't we each have our own planet to live on? Life is a divine plan and an essential aspect of the plan is for humans to learn how to cooperate with each other and the Earth and respect all life in order to create balanced and harmonious living. If we intend to create peace and a quality life on this planet we need to recognize that all life is valuable and recognize our personal responsibility to create a peaceful and safe world.

Everyone on this planet is making a contribution to the evolution of life. Whether you like the experiences in your life or not, somewhere they have purpose as part of the divine plan, which is beyond what our conscious minds can even conceive of. Each person is playing their part in order for the hologram of life to be revealed.

In this cycle, the young child within you merges with the developing adult and you have the opportunity to unite your experiences and passion to go beyond your conditioning and reach for your greatest potential.

What you can feel you can heal.

What you can recognize you can direct.

Trillions of cells working together in our body lets us know there is a system that supports life through cooperation, beyond what we know and understand. Scientifically and metaphysically we are gaining great insights into the unknown universe of our physical bodies and what we discover is "what we don't know". This creates the passion to know more. This cycle uses that passion of seeking more awareness to serve the greatest and highest good for all life on this planet and in the universe.

FOCUS

- **Responsibility**

  Your ability to respond to life rather than react. Be self-referencing in order to respond to life from your own truth.

- **Unity**

  For every action, there is a reaction. All life is interconnected, we are not isolated expressions as humans, your life and the choices you enact make a difference in this world.

- **Courage**

  Rely on your innate courage residing in your heart and soul to guide your choices and decisions in your life, and support your steps of action for change.

GUIDELINES & QUESTIONS

1. What is your focus in this life cycle?

2. List 5 qualities that you developed or choose to develop during this cycle.

3. How are you using the power of this cycle in your life right now?

4. What life patterns or habits did you start using in this cycle that you were unaware until now?

5. What has been the advantage or disadvantage of developing these patterns or habits in your life?

6. Do you value your sexuality? Do you feel safe with your sexuality?

7. Do you value your creativity? Do you feel safe with your creativity?

20 to 22½ Years

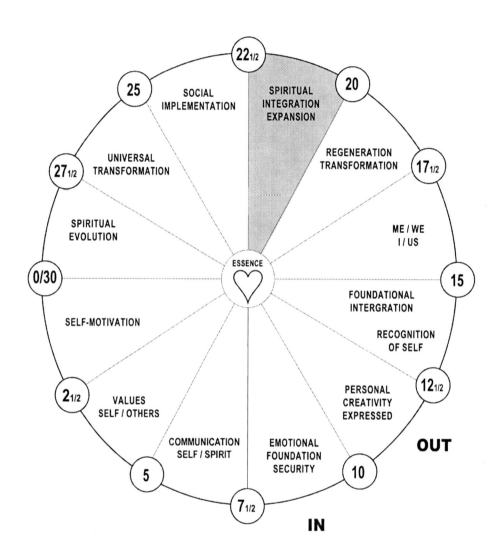

THEME

Inspiration
International awareness
Natural rhythm

Chapter 12

Inspiration

POWER

All life seeks the Light. As a human being, there is an eternal part of you that is always seeking a better way to live, to be happy, to be free of suffering, to make a difference in life. Each person is unique in their quest for these qualities of life- experiences and conditions that will bring us hope, value, recognition and a sense of peaceful purpose.

During this cycle of life, your inspiration comes on strongly as a guiding factor for your choices in life. Having just come through the cycle of transformation of your power, personally and collectively, you emerge with a desire to direct that power in meaningful ways that will influence life on a large scale. This cycle provides a natural window of expanded awareness that is easily accessible if you are willing to question your beliefs and choices in life in relationship to your essential truth in your heart.

Your innate self, your soul, knows you are interconnected with all life regardless of what conditioned beliefs you have received in growing up. Any illusion of separation from your soul and the oneness of life will directly contribute to the level of stress you experience in your daily life. Every breath is your connection to all life, to your soul. It is impossible to be "alive" and be separated from your soul, or any other life forms. Divorcing yourself from the illusion of separation is one of the most powerful gifts you can give to your self and this planet.

VULNERABILITY

Since our educational systems are designed to focus on the linear and academic process of learning (1/8 trained mind), there is no support to explore and investigate the non-linear abstract reality (7/8 natural mind), where all creation takes place. Thus you may have grown up disregarding your intuition and inner awareness as valuable because it is not tangible in the way you were taught to recognize daily reality. During this cycle of your life, your intuition and inner awareness once again seeks to be recognized as a constant influence in your life. When this inner partnership of your mind and heart is present, this is your true soul mate.

This is the time in your life when your intuition and inner awareness begin to generate changes in your thinking through creating doubt, questions, cynicism, changing values, etc. in relationship to your current mental reality. If you don't question your reality, your beliefs systems, your behavior, your relationships in life, your creative life force will be stagnate. Movement and change is life. If you maintain your curiosity, spontaneity, and childlike enthusiasm your mind is always open to new possibilities in life, and the aliveness that comes with it. If you become too linear, you diminish your relationship with this creative childlike energy that is always seeking expression in new ways.

DISCOVERIES

To make changes in your life requires changing your thinking so you can make different choices and take different actions in your daily life. You do not have to make a giant leap in consciousness to make a significant change in your life. Baby steps work. . . and sometimes they are much easier because you can adjust to the changes you initiate, and allow yourself the opportunity to monitor the movement and the direction you are going. All changes occur from the inside out. Your response to life will determine your experience to any given situation; how you will participate and with what quality you experience the event.

In this cycle, your soul is calling you to go beyond the man-made laws and beliefs, transcend the conditioned thinking and soar above the "norm", allowing your soul to guide you to new dimensions of thinking and believing in yourself, others and life in general.

This is a very inspirational cycle and as a result of your mental questioning that usually comes into your life during this cycle, it could bring with it some sense of confusion.

Confusion is not an emotion. It is a state of transformation that occurs just prior to the conscious mind accepting or trying to reject an emerging expression from your soul. Do not try and "get rid of" the confusion, just allow it to be there, it is destined to disappear as the emerging wisdom comes into conscious recognition it will fade like the dawn at high noon.

DIRECTIVES

Confusion precedes clarity and is the messenger that indicates change is coming. When your conscious mind (1/8) can create questions, your sub-conscious mind (7/8) already has an answer – some news to deliver to your consciousness. Whenever you begin to question your beliefs, your life, your values, etc., you are being encouraged by your soul to open up to new ways of living. Change occurs when you are opening up new avenues of thinking, believing or behaving. You cannot have change in your life if everything remains comfortable and familiar, that is why curiosity is such a powerful quality for creativity and aliveness in life. The energy of this cycle is very magnetic, inviting you to receive new ideas and greater blessings in your life.

Unfamiliar and unknown experiences usually feel uncomfortable and generate fear. Fear is a bio-chemical response activated by the limbic part of the brain any time your conscious mind does not recognize an experience or condition in your life as familiar. There will be a chemical activation of the adrenals producing cortisol and preparing your body to be ready to "fight or flight". If this energy does not get used for extreme physical movement and remains in your system, the cortisol is very toxic so you need to assist it to move out of your body, mentally, physically, and emotionally.

Erase your forehead, from the center out towards your temples, several times, saying,

"I release any energy that darkens my own light". Following this tap on your thymus, which is a small gland under your breastbone (sternum) located at the heart level. While tapping on your breastbone, several times with good strong taps, say repeatedly as you tap, "I deeply love and appreciate myself".

Now drink some water. You can consciously support your autonomic nervous system to respond in a different way by working directly with your neurological system. Anytime you feel stress, take several deep breaths right away and drink some water. You will be amazed how these two choices will support your body, mind and emotions immediately.

Enthusiasm is the fuel for this exploration of consciousness. Enthusiasm comes from a word that means "god within". Be sure and check your feelings when you think you feel frightened: could it really be the power of enthusiasm moving through your body instead of fear? There is a good possibility you are more accustomed to the feeling of fear than enthusiasm. They both have the power to support you to make great changes. Take a moment when these feelings arise and really ask what the feelings represent. Do not allow yourself to become habituated to your uncomfortable feelings always being fear, when there are many variations of emotions that are spawned by new events in life, other than just fear.

We have a tendency in the western society to use anger and fear as a garbage pail for all emotions. . . .just dump everything into those two buckets, regardless of what the true expression might be. Don't allow yourself to fall into that trap. You will not only waste a lot of energy by ignoring the true feelings you have, you will miss out many times on lovely life fulfilling experiences because you just "dumped" all the emotions into the familiar containers called fear or anger.

In every generation, inspiration and enthusiasm are the fuel for change in consciousness to go beyond the structures, doctrines, dogma, and systems in life and find a new path for all humanity. The magnetism for change in this cycle is not just a personal fulfillment. Your soul is calling you to make your personal exploration so you can contribute your awareness to the whole of humanity. It is essential that what you discover, you trust, so you have confidence to explore the possibilities that you are uncovering and to go beyond your personal reality and explore the unified field of humanity and all life.

What goes on in this cycle will enhance your awareness of other cultures, other philosophies, and other possibilities. During this time, in spite of what appears to be tremendous differences in lifestyles on the planet, the common denominator emerges, all the ways in which humans are alike. We all need to feel safe, loved and wanted and we all need to be seen, heard and recognized, each in our own way. Change takes place from the inside out, whether within your own life, family life, community, or the government. Everything must change, because that is the energy of all life. Consciously support life and living.

FOCUS

- **Truth**

  Your innate Self recognizes the wisdom of the ages and is seeking an expression through your life now.

- **Receptivity**

  Nothing new is born from constriction. Open your heart and mind to receive the universal awareness that lives within you.

- **Joy**

  Joy is an abiding experience in your heart and soul and constantly seeks expression in your life. Accept this gift of life now.

GUIDELINES & QUESTIONS

1. List 3 beliefs you have/had at this age that need to change because you changed.

2. How will changing these beliefs affect your life?

3. What kind of support or activities do you need to engage in to make this transition easy for you?

4. How will these changes affect your partner? children? parents? community?

5. What is it you have been preparing your whole life to do?

6. What is the cost of your aliveness if you do not do it?

22½ to 25 Years

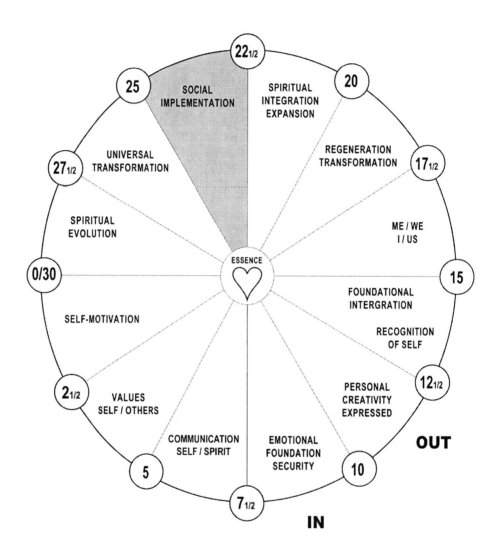

THEME

Career/ Profession
How you are seen in the world
Outlet for your creativity

Chapter 13

Public Identity

POWER

At this age, your presentation in the world is important to you. Your energy and creativity are ready to be demonstrated and shared with others. Your self-confidence to express yourself is stronger and based on your emotional foundation developed during the ages of 7½ to 10. Any places in your life where your emotional foundation is vulnerable or empty will have a big influence in your work/professional life at this time. Your emotional stability and self-confidence is the foundation for putting your creativity out into the world. It takes courage, passion and vision to create your professional life and either use a structure already created, such as a company, or create the structure necessary to support your visions and dreams becoming a reality, by being an entrepreneur.

With a multitude of choices for your career, it is important for you to listen to your heart's desires, otherwise your mental programming will take over and begin to minimize or question your desires and possibilities. This is a really important time to use your personal power gained in the cycle from 20 - 22½ that supported you to claim your personal truth, values and spiritual inspiration. These values are your guiding power for directing your heart and mind, enhanced by your experience and education, and using the skills and tools learned from your life interests. It is helpful at this time to allow yourself to merely create *the next step in your life*, rather than feel like you have to create your whole future in this moment.

The cycle from 20 - 22½ invites your perception to go beyond the man-made laws, seeking the greater wisdom and vision of life for the human potential. This cycle from 22½ to 25 supports working within the structure and tradition of business, organizations, education, government, etc. Learning to walk your talk. The challenge with integrating these two cycles is to listen to your heart and passion, and be willing to go beyond your fears or your limitations to create the system, organization or company that can truly represent your vision and dreams for your future. Entrepreneurs are prevalent today because this is exactly what they are doing: creating businesses that match the way they want to create and live in the world, not working where they feel minimized in their creative expression or have their values compromised just for money or position.

VUNERABILITY

From the time you were very young, you were trained to be responsive and concerned about "other people's" attitudes and behaviors towards you. This feedback formatted the way you relate to yourself today. This is an important social skill to have as long as it does not become your basis for your value in life. Throughout your life, being other-oriented rather that self-referenced, influences you and your choices are based on what others think of you rather than your listening to your own heart and soul. Being other-oriented in referencing your choices influences your sense of self-confidence and self-esteem and undermines trusting what you really intuitively know and want. When you learn to self-reference in your life you listen to your heart and soul and make choices to take steps of action that support those desires. This is not being selfish, this is being self-responsible to fulfill your soul commitment.

If you have gone to college right after high school, you have recently graduated from the educational system that has organized your life for 12 - 16 years. Now you no longer have that structure to rely on, and you may be new to your profession or skills. Today's choices are so diversified -- from agriculture to global technology -- that to organize your skills, potential career opportunities, and your emotional foundation all at the same time can seem overwhelming. Coupled with the requirement that for many jobs they want you have a certain degree **and** previous experience. These conditions can feel like you are in a no-win situation.

The desire you have to express yourself and your creativity is influenced by your emotional foundation, created between 7½ and 10. Wounded or empty places in your emotional life during that age can create defensive or withdrawn behaviors based on fears. These behaviors act as an emotional "leak" in your life and will influence the loss of power in your business life until you heal the wounded areas and/or fill up your emotional tank. Self-confidence in this cycle becomes even more apparent as you start putting your ideas out in the business world for others to see; you really realize your level of vulnerability in exposing your visions and creativity to others' responses and possible criticism.

DISCOVERIES

Everything is energy and information. All life is interconnected and energy is always moving and changing and needs space for movement and expression. One of the challenges and blessings of this cycle in your life is allowing yourself to go beyond the history or tradition of your training in life and create a vehicle or expression that matches your creativity. This is why it is essential to have your heart and mind working in partnership, so you can maintain your balance as you expand your reality to accommodate your visions. Vision and Action are essential partners to accomplish anything as a human being.

DIRECTIVES

During this cycle you are going to be seeking some kind of structure to direct your energy in your life. Your passion and power are high at this age and need appropriate outlets that match the levels of the visions and dreams you have. Since you have many years to increase your productivity, you can experience this time in your life as a "practice time" or a "hallway of life", something you are going through that takes you closer to your intended visions in life. When you live in this cycle with that perspective, you can reduce your frustration and the impatience of having to create *right now* and allow yourself the options of enjoying the journey of creating.

As you experience or review your life during this cycle, filling in some of the empty emotional spaces from 7½ - 10, you can begin to feel more stable and grounded, continuing to create your foundation in life for your career, and draw upon your life experiences. It is important to remember that life is a journey, not a destination and that each discovery, comfortable of uncomfortable, is a blessing to assist you in "moving your energy" to new levels of creativity, more closely aligned with your soul commitments. Every choice you make and every decision you create is a stepping-stone getting you closer and closer to your wisdom and visions.

FOCUS

- **Listen to your heart**

  If you do not listen to your heart, no matter what you do or how successful you appear you will not feel fulfilled, because your heart's desires will be unfulfilled.

- **Self-reference**

  You have a commitment to bring your special and unique gifts to life, and you cannot do that if you do not honor your inner wisdom and guidance.

- **Trust yourself**

  Your link to life is through your heart and soul. If you don't trust yourself in this primary relationship, all other life experiences will be tainted with your lack of trust in yourself.

GUIDELINES & QUESTIONS

1. Name three things that are missing for you emotionally that influence your stability in your career.

2. How do you want to feel in your career?

3. Do you have trust in yourself to receive your visions and create your dreams for the future?

4. If not, why not? What interferes with your trusting yourself?

5. What are five things that excite you about your future?

6. What is the first step you are going to take today to begin your journey to create the future you desire?

25 to 27½ Years

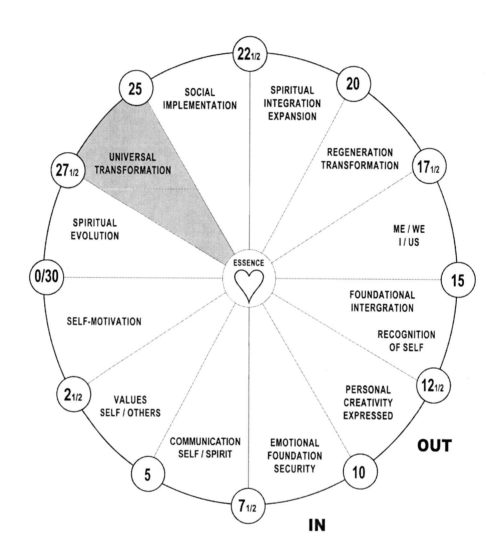

THEME

Humanitarian needs
Global Family awareness
Transformation

Chapter 14

Universal Awareness

POWER

A dream is a wish your heart makes. . . . Consciously or unconsciously you are motivated by the dreams in your heart, because this is your soul calling you to remember and meet your agreements and promises for your soul's expression in your human experience. Many times, until the dream calls you consciously, you feel unfilled with a subtle sense of unrest and a questing in life that has no satisfaction from the outside consumer-driven reality.

In your heart you know you are part of a "bigger plan". Breathing is a daily clue you are connected to something invisible and bigger than your mind can understand. From 10 - 12½, your heart was already in touch with the desire to express yourself in a bigger way through your personal creativity. Whatever experiences you had at that age, were a preview of a bigger stage in life involving humanity. You are a part of a global family, simply because you were born. This is the time, from 25 - 27½, to consciously explore your relationship with the collective family of humanity and recognize and claim your innate gift that is influencing the evolution of humanity.

You are part of the global family: color, creed, culture, religion, or gender does not divide this family. We are united through the heart and soul of life. We all are sharing the same breath with each other and all other life. You can create the illusion of separation in your mind, but all life is interconnected and the connection cannot be broken. This awareness has become the foundation for Quantum Physics, which is a huge change in collective consciousness from Newton's Law of Physics. This is called Oneness, the unified field, which Einstein devoted the last 30 years of his life to.

As a part of the global family, the most important contribution you can make is YOU:

the truth of you, the love that you are, the unique gifts that only you can give. There is no Xerox copy of you. You are the only one wearing your fingerprints, your soul blueprint. Now is the time to accept this truth about you. You are important to the evolution of the species and no one else can make your contribution. This is not a burden this is a privilege. You are a chosen one. *You* chose to be on planet earth and make your contribution at this time.

VULNERABILITY

Giving yourself permission to expand your sense of global family you can begin to relate to the dreams lying dormant within your heart. These dreams have been waiting until the collective consciousness was available and are now beginning to stretch and emerge as conscious ideas and demonstrations in your life. This is birthing yourself, acknowledging your potential and becoming your active creative expression – revealing to the world who you really are.

The stretch and expansion of consciousness that takes place in this cycle will open your eyes, your mind, your belief systems and your receptivity to creation in such a deep and powerful way, you will never see the world in the same way again. Sometimes the experience in this cycle is really deep and subtle. Sometimes it is dramatic and chaotic. The purpose is the same: to expand your life to include the bigger picture of the divine plan that you are representing through your personal life.

This is the true meaning of "ownership and integrity." This is an inside job. When you claim you are a co-creator with all life, you begin to own your divinity and when that occurs, your life will be motivated from the inside out, through your heart and soul. Integrity begins with this divine marriage of your mind, your heart and your soul--the trinity within--functioning as a team. Making conscious choices, with your heart and mind as partners, supports your inner truth and completely changes the quality of life you live, whether the environment and people change or not.

All energy of this cycle is designed to support your releasing limitations, constrictions, conditioning, and illusions of who you are so the "bud" that you have been can now fully "blossom". Something has to give, in order for you, the bud, to be released to the full blossom you are intended to be. Releasing may feel like loss. Remember that releasing is allowing that which is greater within you to emerge so it is different from loss and can actually bring comfort and fulfillment to you as you unfold your soul's purpose.

DISCOVERIES

In this cycle, your consciousness naturally expands and greater recognition of the extended global family begins to seep into your reality, your daily life. You may be more responsive to news that involves the rest of the world than ever before, especially with the Internet available to the masses now. The cyberspace connection may begin to have a deeper impact on you than you realize because the news that comes to you from around the world is now part of your daily life: it is bigger than you imagined and moving faster most of the time than you can understand. In today's world you must think differently, and learn a new language that applies to this changing world of communication.

Einstein spent the last 30 years of his life working with the unified field. Now, 50 years later, this is no longer a theory but becoming a more conscious way of life. We are a global family and our home is on Mother Earth. Working together as a family, we can truly begin to demonstrate what the indigenous tribes have known for generations; make choices that will influence life seven generations from now. The future starts now, with you and me and our personal family.

DIRECTIVES

It is helpful when you look at how we humans are behaving in the world today to remember that all life is created in the force field of love: the world is created from the inside out, not the outside in. Being clear and truthful with your self is the foundation for creating balanced living.

How we, as individuals, chose to behave is our personal responsibility, not a divine plan. The choices we make determine the experiences we have in our life. If you are confused about what is happening inside of you, you will carry confusion as part of your life and can experience that reality wherever you go. Remember, confusion precedes clarity. This is the price of being a species that has a free will to co-create; because everything is interconnected we influence all life with each choice we make.

The sun and the moon represent two different aspects of each day. All life has different views of reality. Do not get caught in thinking everything is only daylight or darkness. Each day is both. All life is both the light and the dark, living with purpose and meaning beyond our limited conscious perception. The purpose of this cycle is to open your thinking until both the light and the dark of life are living as oneness in your reality, not a polarity. Everything is a part of the divine plan.

Go beyond trying to understand. Understanding is a booby prize. Participate in your life as an open book, observing life and being open to all the changes taking place as part of a divine plan. This does not mean you have to like all the changes, agree with them, or even want to participate in them, and yet, all change influences each and every one of us. Consciously choosing to create a quality of life for yourself and making your contribution to the planet activates your personal responsibility for your part in the whole picture. This cycle stretches your humanness so your divinity has room to be born.

FOCUS

- **Collective awareness**

  We are interconnected with all life; we all share the same breath. You need to be conscious of your choices and the long-range influence for you personally and collectively.

- **Personal responsibility**

  Do not take life personally and be personally responsible for your life and your choices.

- **You are a gift**

  When you recognize and claim your innate abilities and purpose on this planet you can increase your conscious contribution to humanity, fulfilling your soul purpose.

GUIDELINES & QUESTIONS

1. Why did you choose to come to planet earth?
2. What is your contribution to life?
3. Is it time for you to consciously increase your contribution to life?
4. What do you need to change in order to do that?
5. What support do you want as you expand your reality and beliefs?
6. What is the dream that lives in your heart?
7. Do you trust yourself to tell yourself the truth and listen to what you know?

27½ to 30 Years

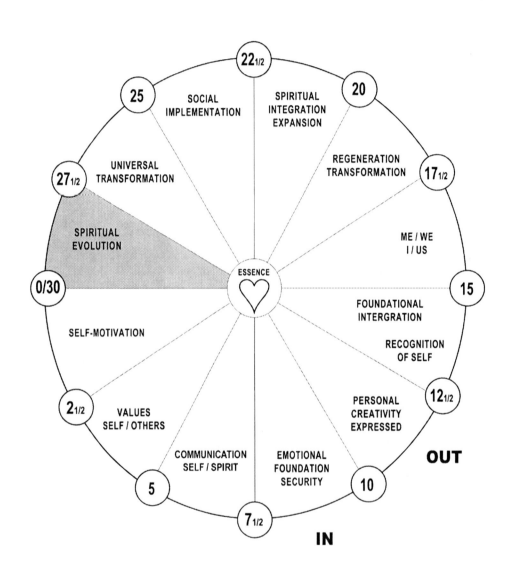

THEME

Chrysalis
New life
Spiritual power

Chapter 15

Spiritual Foundation

POWER

It is time to be born again, consciously. You re-enter the womb of spirit to begin an inner inventory of your experiences you have created for yourself during the first 27½ years of your life. You are unconsciously, and sometimes consciously, examining the foundation you are preparing for the next 30 years of your life. This cycle is a clearing and sorting out of everything that does not fit your intended future, based on your heart and soul wisdom. This sorting and clearing will influence every level of your thinking, your beliefs, your philosophy, your relationships, your work, your family ties, your life experiences and how they have influenced you. You will be reviewing your choices that created those life experiences, your relationship with spirit, your relationship with money and your body--every area of your life is up for review, and revision or transformation if needed.

The level of expansion you accept and allow to happen for yourself during this cycle from 25 - 27½ deeply influences your comfort level in your life at this time. The more you allow yourself to release and expand, the more comfortable you are in giving birth to yourself in this cycle. If you resist the changes your body and your life will reflect the constriction. Give yourself permission to release yourself to the flow of life and you can experience relief and less stress in your life. Now is the time to do what is needed to make changes in your life. If you show up consciously and responsibly for yourself, you can choose what will support you right now and will influence your future as well.

Accept the privilege it is to be a conscious co-creator in your life. When you were in the womb being created as a baby, your soul was the guiding force for your experience. Your soul still is the guiding force and now you can consciously cooperate with your soul wisdom and actively intend your future by the choices you make today. This is truly the gift of co-creating and it is innate and yours every moment in your life.

VULNERABILITY

This cycle in your life is kind of like the rumblings of an earthquake; everything inside and outside is being shaken and changing. This is a natural process at this age because this is a time of tremendous change and review. You may have many new experiences available to you, increasing your options and choices for the life you are creating. Remember you are sorting what has been in your life and what is coming in. Give yourself permission to change your mind many times about major and minor things in life. That is natural and the purpose of this cycle in your life.

Expect your emotions to be as changeable as your mind. This is truly a roller coaster ride emotionally because so much that was familiar is being disassembled or remodeled. You base your identity and security on what is familiar. You could feel fearful of the unknown or unfamiliar, even though these conditions are a part of the natural evolution of your life. Whatever you feel during this cycle of change is OK. Do not judge yourself because you are so "emotional". Emotions are the fuel for movement. You need a lot of fuel for the movement you are in. This is a birth for your new life. Making a new foundation for life requires a lot of power, movement and action. Your emotions provide the fuel for the launch.

DISCOVERIES

Think BIG!! This is the time to plan and focus your attention, desires, dreams and visions with a very expansive view of all that is possible. The more you are willing to allow your current foundation to disassemble and reassemble in a new way, the easier it is for you to co-create the future you are intending. This is the time to truly be in harmony and united with your heart and soul. All parts of you need a voice in this remodel. . . . mind, emotions, body, heart and soul. You are going to cohabit with all these parts of yourself for the rest of your life. If each part is recognized and respected during such a major juncture in your life you are more assured of greater peace and harmony in your daily life.

Your conscious mind is completely trainable anytime during your life so when you want a new program, change the "software". Provide a new format and direction to your conscious and unconscious mind through the choices you make, and you can open up new pathways for new thought patterns. This is called reticular activation. Kind of like when you buy a new car. . . now everywhere you go you see that brand of car. Thoughts are like that. Whatever you decide to bring into focus in your conscious mind will attract the power and energy that matches those thoughts. Thoughts are a magnetic energy that draws to you whatever you focus on. Your power goes where your thoughts flow and your power returns to you on the same path you sent the thoughts out on. Conscious, responsible thinking is essential to change your future for yourself and our children.

If you become a parent during this cycle, your child has come in as your teacher and guide during your life. Throughout your life you will be in the same cycles at least part of the time. The children are our future and your child will be the doorway for you to new possibilities to learn and grow together. This path together can be one of great comfort and guidance by respecting your child as a teacher/guide. If you are confined and constricted in old beliefs that may not be authentic for you, this relationship could be the one that challenges your core values and beliefs until you claim your own deep inner truth. Either way, this relationship is a great blessing for you and your child. It may not always feel easy or as if it is a blessing and time will assist this recognition for both of you.

If you marry during this cycle the marriage is designed to encourage growth and change, since that is the foundation on which it was created. Growth and change is not always comfortable so it is important to know that this is a foundational aspect of your marriage, a soul agreement, and you can appreciate the opportunities of this marriage with greater awareness. Relationship is a classroom for greater self-awareness, and your marriage will be supportive of your personal and soul commitments of learning new ways to relate. Always refer to and remember the love that called you into relationship, no matter what the trials of relating may present.

DIRECTIVES

It is essential that you are kind, patient and loving with yourself during this cycle. You are going to make many decisions and change your mind a lot and feel "up, down, and all around" emotionally. All of this is *normal* for this cycle. You will feel a greater sense of ease and comfort during this cycle if you don't bring in the JUDGE! It is already challenging enough to manage all the change, let alone to judge yourself.

Make a contract with the part of yourself that is the Judge. Give the judge a conscious presence. Place your left hand above your left shoulder, open like you are saying a pledge, and identify this as the Judge. Speak out loud, thanking the Judge for all the years of good service, paying attention to all the details, making decisions, and being consistent in your life. Notify the Judge that this position is closed. You no longer need a Judge.

Now, above your right shoulder, place your right hand, open position, and name this position the Director. Invite the Judge to become your new Director. In this new position, you want the Judge to be as discerning, pay attention to all the details, be as consistent and loyal as before. As the Director, you inform the Judge that judgments are no longer allowed and what you are requesting is an observer in your life to assist the Director, gather and report new information and encourage your changes in life from a positive view. The Director position, with the assistance of the observer, is to give you the news of the moment and leave out the judgments based on the past. This partnership gives you the details so you can make your decisions based on what is true for you, as your heart and mind seek to be in partnership.

Everything is possible. If your mind and heart can conceive or believe, you can create it. Enjoy the expansion, vulnerability, revelations, discoveries, memories, joys, sadness, triumphs, disappointments, hopes and visions of this cycle. You are emerging as a brand new Being, for another grand cycle of this wondrous life. Enjoy - In Joy.

FOCUS

- **Inner awareness**

  Honor your inner awareness and the support that is available as you sort out your life.

- **Be respectful of your process**

  This is one of the more important cycles in your life so allow yourself to have the feelings, fears, questions, doubts, confusion, joy, hope, visions of this change.

- **Be courageous**

  Many things are changing and rearranging in your life right now. Do not feel that you have to make big decisions at this time unless life demands that from you. Give yourself time to be born anew at 30.

GUIDELINES & QUESTIONS

1. What are your major strengths in your life?

2. What are your challenges, vulnerability, and weak points you want to change now?

3. What is your level of trust of yourself? your soul?

4. How does this influence your trust of life? others?

5. What do you desire to create and change now to go forward in life with confidence and enthusiasm?

6. What does "quality of life" mean to you?

7. How can you create a life that matches these qualities?

8. Are you ready to take the steps of action to do that? If not, why not?

9. What is it you have prepared your whole life to do?

10. What is the cost if you do not do it?

Implementation

Second 30 Year Cycle

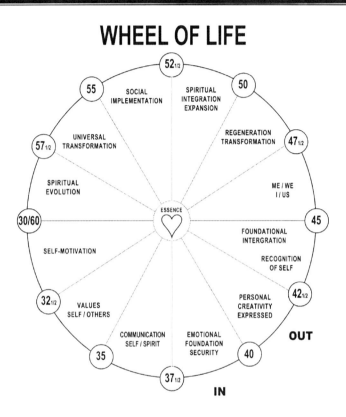

WHEEL OF LIFE

(Wheel labels, clockwise from top)

52½
55 — SOCIAL IMPLEMENTATION
50
SPIRITUAL INTEGRATION EXPANSION
47½ — REGENERATION TRANSFORMATION
57½ — UNIVERSAL TRANSFORMATION
ME / WE I / US
SPIRITUAL EVOLUTION
45
30/60
FOUNDATIONAL INTERGRATION
RECOGNITION OF SELF
SELF-MOTIVATION
42½ — PERSONAL CREATIVITY EXPRESSED
32½ — VALUES SELF / OTHERS
OUT
COMMUNICATION SELF / SPIRIT
EMOTIONAL FOUNDATION SECURITY
35
40
37½
IN
ESSENCE ♡

30 to 60-years

Implementation - now is the time to walk your talk, and deliver to life the gifts, talents and abilities that you have acquired, honed, practiced and prepared from the first thirty-year cycle. Planning for a safari is one thing; going on the safari is the experience. If we were more conscious, as a species, of the preparations we make every day and in every cycle in our life for our future, we would have a much bigger picture of what kind of future we are investing in for ourselves and our children.

30 to 32½ Years

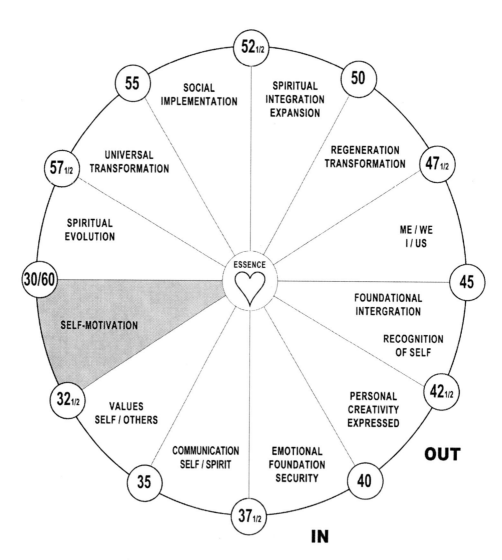

THEME

Personal identity
Personal fulfillment
Self-referencing

Chapter 16

Attention & Motivation

POWER

This is the cycle that creates the structure you will use to get attention, recognize your self-identity and motivation during the next 30 years of your life. No matter how you developed during this cycle from birth to 2½, you can make conscious decisions now in recognition of who you are and the ways in which you choose to get your needs met that support your integrity and intentions in your life.

These are good questions to ask of your self in this cycle:

- How do I want to create my life now to get the attention I want and deserve?
- What motivates me in life?
- Who am I?

As an infant, you were not consciously asking yourself these questions any more than you were consciously asking yourself when you were going to walk and talk, even though that is also part of your divine plan as a human being. Review this last 30 years as a spiral that brought you to this same cycle and yet your view of "You" is expanded because you have many experiences and memories that have influenced your reality, behavior, beliefs, and choices. Consciousness increases your receptivity and participation in life at whatever level you choose to "play the game of life". In the Universe, you always have another chance because life is an evolutionary process not a destination. Relax and pay attention to your life right now and know that change is just a choice away under any conditions you might experience.

VULNERABILITY

You have just completed a thorough foundational review from 27½ - 30 years old preparing you for this opportunity of consciously creating a new life for yourself and making choices that can be more congruent with who you are now. Thirty years of living gives you a good clue about what works and what doesn't work in your life and yet this time can feel so new and unfamiliar that you really don't have a lot of confidence in what to do next.

You start this next 30 years in the same cycle as when you were born. (See Chapter 4) Give yourself permission to go slowly and take baby steps in making choices and allowing yourself time to adjust to the renewed foundation you are creating. An important consideration for deciding which choices you make is based on what kind of life you want for yourself, now that you get to consciously co-create it. If you go on a road trip, you usually have some kind of trip plan and a road map. On the journey you may completely change your plans and route, and you still have to start somewhere and have some destination or desire in mind.

Life is like that. You need to know where you are and where are you intending to go, so you can make your choices and measure your movement to make sure you are heading in the direction you are intending. You can always change your mind, you just need to decide and begin moving your feet. Aliveness is movement and change.

DISCOVERIES

Everything is energy and information: where your focus goes your power flows. This is not common knowledge taught in school. Until you become aware of the power of your thinking and realize that your life experiences really do have something to do with your reality; your thoughts, your desires, your fears, your doubts, your faith, your trust, your family patterns, your social conditioning, your environment, and your sense of safety in the world you can feel like a victim or less powerful than you really are.

If you recognize this cycle in your life as a birth, that you really are "starting anew" at age 30 and have the advantage now that you can employ conscious choices this time in your life and you can feel excited as well as frightened. Even though you have had experiences that influenced your sense of trust, confidence, and self-esteem before, the way you sort your information in life influences the choices you make and creates the difference in your comfort level and satisfaction of truly creating what you desire. You do not have to repeat the choices or patterns of the last thirty years if you are willing to consciously sort your options in life now. This takes courage and patience and perseverance and the reward is HUGE!!

DIRECTIVES

I suggest using this simple **MENTAL INVENTORY** tool of support for sorting the options in your life. Without editing, write down ALL the things in your life that are NOT working for you right now under **LIABILITIES**. **Burn this list the same day written.**

When you consciously recognize what is not working, you give your subconscious mind permission to release these concerns and conditions and make way for new choices. If the pitcher is full, there is no room to put anything else in. Empty it out and you can always refill it with what you want.

List all the things in your life under **ASSETS** that are working for you and that you feel grateful for. Keep this list and continue to add to it.

WHAT'S MISSING?

You can now assess what is missing in your life and with conscious recognition you can focus on obtaining your intentions. When you can recognize what you want, then you can begin to create a plan to direct your energy, intention and consciousness to create that desire and take the necessary steps of action to support that happening.

Since you are just starting a new 30-year cycle, this is a good time to use the Mental

Inventory and determine your intentions for this 2½-year cycle, where you are now, and where you would like to be in 7½ years, and in 15 years. This takes you half way through the next 30-year cycle and can be supportive to enlarge your picture and potential for your life by making choices that will support you on a long-range basis. Be willing to let these choices change and expand as you move through your life experiences. You are not limited by your last 30 years unless you allow yourself to be. This is a new beginning for you and you can create a new way of living in this next 30 years if you have the courage to choose what you really want and take steps of action to create it. Grace in life always provides many chances to continue to grow in a more balanced and healthy way if you want to make that choice.

FOCUS

- **Trust**

  Trust that your life experiences have revealed to you the areas of satisfaction and dissatisfaction and you can influence this balance in your life by the choices you make today.

- **Courage**

  This is a new life: have the courage to make different choices than you have ever made before and listen to your heart as a guiding force in making your choices.

- **Excitement**

  Concentrate on the excitement of this great adventure, your life, and have fun everyday trying new ideas, options, and lifestyles, even in the smallest way.

QUESTIONS AND GUIDELINES

1. How do you seek to get attention in your life now?

2. Does this attention satisfy and fulfill you?

3. If not, why not and what do you want to do to change that?

4. Describe 5 - 10 qualities that you recognize you have obtained over the last 30 years that you admire in yourself.

5. Describe 5 - 10 habits, beliefs or behaviors that you recognize you have obtained over the last 30 years that you do not admire in yourself.

6. What choices do you need to make and what action do you need to take to change these qualities into ones that you can admire?

32½ to 35 Years

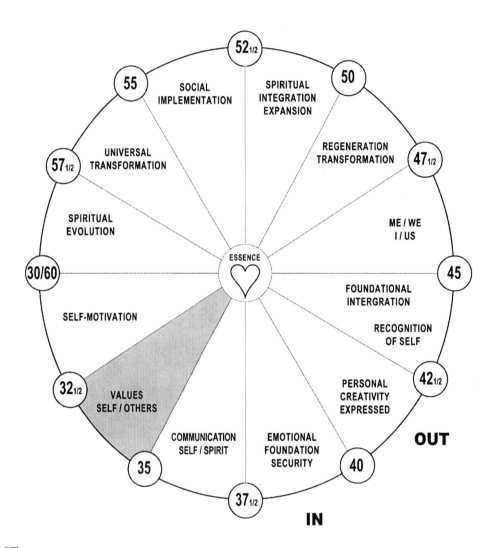

THEME

    Personal Value
        Values in life
    Self-recognition
        Sexuality

Chapter 17

Values

POWER

Now that you have made some choices about what kind of foundation you want to develop for your future, these choices influence the value system you will be using for the next 30 years as well. The values you developed and have used since you were 2½ - 5 years old were created by the way you were treated as you interacted with those around you at that age. This value system was the basis of your sense of self-confidence and self-esteem as you went through the cycles of life until this age.

A value system that is based on the way you are treated or recognized by others sets up a pattern of using outside conditions to determine your value and qualify you and your experiences in life. There is no consistency or stability in this reference system. Everything and everyone around you is constantly changing. This kind of referencing creates a lot of doubt about yourself and your feelings. The value of who you are is not based on what is "outside of you," rather what is "inside of you". This is the difference of being outer-referenced or inner-referenced, self-referenced.

This cycle in life is a significant time of assessing your value system from inside of you, rather than outside of you. The most important thing in life is not how others feel about you or how they treat you, it is how do you feel about you and how do you treat yourself? Until you get clear on this, you can never stabilize your self-esteem and self-confidence which is strengthened by listening to your inner awareness, your desires and trusting who you are, no matter how others relate to you.

VULNERABILITY

Since you have had 32½ years practicing an *outer-referenced* value system, developing an *inner-referenced* value system does not happen overnight, and it will not take another 32½ years. The main thing is to be patient with yourself in this process of change because your value system is foundational and must change organically to support enhancing your stability in a natural way.

As you develop your inner value system, this encourages your ability to access your soul blueprint where your innate life skills, talents and abilities are latent. You cannot receive the creativity of your own innate abilities if you are lacking in self-love or self-confidence, which are necessary components for your being able to acknowledge your abilities as well as have the confidence to express and experience them.

When you consciously begin to access your values, you will be able to notice how they have changed, or not, during the last 32½ years, and what quality of life you developed that has been influenced by your original value system. Now is the time to have your value system congruent with your intentions and desires so you can create the life that is meaningful and fulfilling for you, from the inside out. This is the only way you will ever have confidence in yourself and trust your choices in life to guide you to your highest expression and creativity.

DISCOVERIES

In an outer-based value system, the emphasis is on appearance and opinion of others. In an inner-based value system, the emphasis is based on your inner knowing, your intuition, personal truth and heart's desire. As you develop your foundation that you will use through the next 30-year cycle, it is very important to have a relationship with your own heart's desires and personal aspirations to support guiding your intentions and create the life that you are capable of expressing.

An outer-based value system continues to enroll you in the stereotypes of the collective consciousness that evaluates your beauty, talents, skill, abilities, intelligence, personal value, etc. as a consumer to enroll you to continue purchasing "something" to make you "look/feel" better. Since this rarely happens from something you purchase, and even if it does, it is not enduring, consumerism continues in search of the "look good/feel good" reality.

When your inner values do not get to have a voice and be considered as part of your life expression, you will continue to feel a void in your life no matter what you purchase to look and feel good. This cycle is the time to naturally open to deeper levels of awareness of your heart and inner wisdom so you can establish an inner-based value system that honors your soul commitment. When you create your world from the inside out, your life will never be the same and many of the desires that motivated your life before will no longer hold the same interest for you.

DIRECTIVES

In an outer-based value system far too much emphasis is placed on the human self and not the soul and inner wisdom. During this cycle, you will be re-evaluating your relationship with your body, your sexuality, your health and your desire to be comforted and nurtured in life. Affection is attention on a physical level and is deeply satisfying to your heart and soul and transcends logic and nurtures your inner desire to feel safe, loved and wanted. Attention is a primal need throughout our life and physical touch and affection are one of the purest ways to receive attention. It is important that touch and affection be gentle, kind and respectful because of the deep impact on your senses.

Your relationship with your body and your sexuality was strongly imprinted during this cycle 30 years ago when you were potty trained. If you have maintained any lack of respect for your body and all its natural functions, including your sexuality, this is the cycle to redirect that thinking and appreciate your body as the vehicle for your soul. The foundation of your comfort or rejection of your sexuality and creativity was foundationally developed in this cycle 30 years ago.

The energy of your sexuality and spirituality are the same energy; they are the power of the creative life force. Being in denial or disapproval of any part of your body, mind or emotions influences your sense of wholeness, acceptance of yourself and your peace of mind in all areas of your life. Give yourself permission to develop a new or deeper relationship with your own sexuality/spiritually on every level. Allow the right-and-wrong value system that may have been imprinted in your life about your sexuality and your genitals to be transcended by your recognition that your sexuality and spirituality are the same energy and deserve the same reverence, respect and responsibility as every other part of your body.

When you live in your body in love and appreciation for the privilege of having life and realizing how fragile and precious human life is, your reality shifts forever. An inner-based value system is filled with gratitude for all the gifts that are yours in life. Gratitude is a tremendous sorting system to "get real" about what matters and evaluate what you have been taught to see if it is important to you and your heart's desires. What is more important than a healthy body? A significant part of a healthy body is living and being with your heart's desires and taking steps of action to make that relationship a lifestyle.

FOCUS

- **Trust**

  Learn to trust yourself, your needs and your choices in life. You can have what you want and still be cooperative with others.

- **Self-referencing**

  You can choose your method of getting satisfying and fulfilling attention. You are not dependent on others to make that choice for you.

- **Acceptance**

  Accept the truth of who you are as a soul, living as a human being. This releases you from being an emotional slave to others' opinions of you.

QUESTIONS AND GUIDELINES

1. Do you deeply love and appreciate yourself?
2. If not, what is preventing you from loving and appreciating yourself?
3. List 10 qualities that are important to you in your inner-based value system.
4. What are or could be some of the benefits of living from your inner-based values?
5. Have you accepted your sexuality/creativity as part of your divinity?
6. Have you taken responsibility for the power of your sexuality/creativity?
7. If not, why not?

35 to 37½ Years

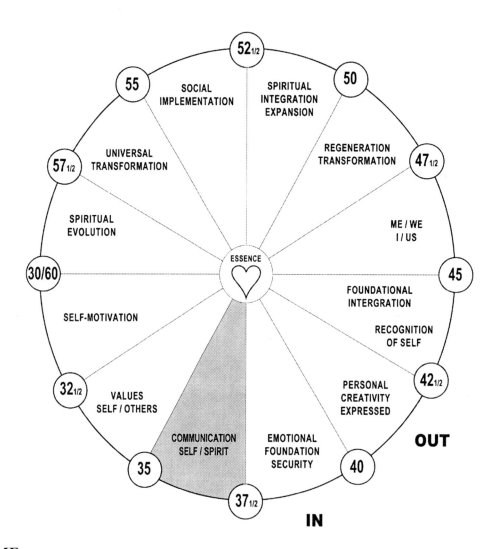

THEME

Communication
Personal
Spiritual
Self-trust

Chapter 18

Communications

POWER

This is a really good time to listen to all those questions you may have been asking about relating to the Universe, the bigger picture of life. The questions are the gateway for your soul to once again reunite with your consciousness and have an active, alive partnership in your daily life. When your conscious mind (1/8) can create a question, the unconscious mind (7/8) already has the answer and guidance available for you. Curiosity and trust are keys to reawakening this partnership and then having the willingness to take the steps of action necessary to make the changes you want to support yourself.

When you claim a new identity and create a new value system for yourself, your relationship with your soul changes. Many of the gray, clouded or illusionary areas of your life begin to clear up, or show up, to be reviewed and/or renewed using your current reality base. Oneness is eternal and always awaits your conscious recognition. The blessing of living as a human being, consciously relating with your soul wisdom, enriches and inspires the quality of your life in spite of the many challenges that human life conditions create.

VULNERABILITY

The major emphasis on "learning", from 5 - 7½ years old, is based on an academic, linear approach to life, disregarding your receptive, intuitive heart and soul as your primary guiding force in life. This creates a schism and a sense of "aloneness or separation" which can compel you throughout your life to seek a sense of "belonging". It is impossible to be separated from your soul, the Essence of who you are; this is an illusion. Yet this conditioning, in our academic world, is so thorough and intense that your heart and soul is may be over-shadowed and cause you to live a "dim" life when in fact you are "bright light", eternally shining through from your soul.

All life seeks the Light. Your eternal quest to shine your Light from your heart and soul is a deep motivating factor for life itself. Even if you have a sense of being alone or lost, this power of Light, seeking itself, will propel you on through harrowing, challenging, and confusing conditions. This is the magnet that continues to call in the breath, even when we are "unconscious" on any level.

DISCOVERIES

This cycle is the time to consciously reunite your human self with your heart and soul to begin to create choices based on the power of this union and notice how differently your "ordinary" life becomes. When you enliven this inner relationship your world begins to be created from the depth of your inner truth rather than outer-referenced fears. Living a self-referenced life allows you to change your reality base in a twinkling of an eye. Everything is energy and encoded information and you are in charge of how you choose to perceive and direct this energy through your beliefs.

As you renew your relationship with your heart and soul, you will discover you are never separated from your innate wisdom and the divine order of the Universe. The illusion of separation comes as a result of your conscious mind being trained to override your heart and soul. Your soul is always communicating with your consciousness and empowering your life to greater wholeness using your heart and intuition as guides for the choices you make daily. All you have to do is listen and receive the guidance. Reuniting your mind with your heart and soul removes the illusion of separation that occurred when your heart and soul got ignored and had no vote in your conscious choices.

DIRECTIVES

During this cycle of reunion between your mind and your heart and soul, use your natural curiosity, innocence and spontaneity to question what you think and what you believe and see how this feels to your heart when you bring up these questions. This is the perfect time in your life to increase your trust and use your heart power to add the peace and joy to your life that you have been seeking since you were a child when this illusion of separation occurred.

When you review your life in this cycle you will probably have some conscious memories of experiences when you were 5½ - 7. Use these memories as a guide to determine the areas of your life where your relationship with your intuition, imagination, and inner voice were diminished or cut off. What part of you is waiting to be reclaimed and released and come alive in your life right now? Give these parts permission to be retrieved and come alive in your world now and discover the joy you have in your wholeness. Rejoice with this reunion of your mind, heart and soul. The heavens ring with gratitude when you allow your divinity to shine through your humanness.

FOCUS

- **Speak up**

  Trust what you think and what you deeply know through your heart and soul connection and share this wisdom with others.

- **Conscious relating**

  You are not alone, you never have been. You are eternally connected to the divine order of all life through your innate inner wisdom. Trust this relationship and live consciously relating to all life.

- **Courage**

Living your truth and speaking your truth is your power. Have the courage to step into your power on a daily basis.

QUESTIONS AND GUIDELINES

1. Did you have invisible playmates when you were a child?
2. How old were you when you "let go" of them?
3. How did you feel when you were told that what you saw or felt was not real?
4. Examine those experiences now and allow them to become real for you again. What does that bring up for you?
5. At what age did you learn to "keep your mouth shut" and not share what you were thinking or feeling?
6. How has this influenced your relationship and trust of your mind and your heart and soul?
7. What do you want to believe in and trust now?

37½ to 40 Years

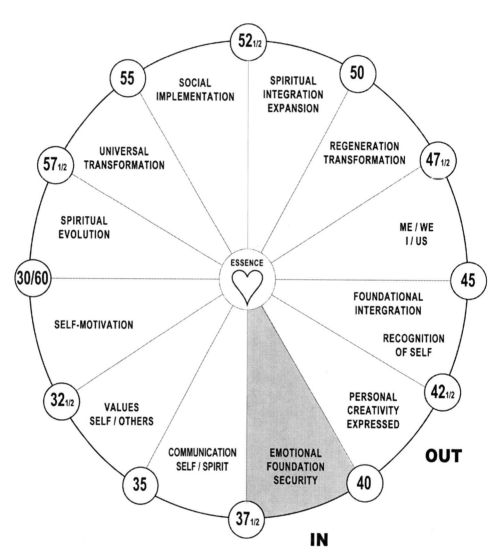

THEME

Emotional transformation
Emotional stability
Emotional needs

Chapter 19

Emotional Foundation

POWER

This age, from 37½ to 40, is one of the most powerful cycles of transformation in your whole life. You can no longer be a "bud". It is time to "blossom". Any conditions, beliefs, experiences, or relationships that are confining or constricting you will be remodeled, or removed during this cycle. Motivated from your soul, your time to expand has come and all parts of your life line up, from the inside out, to initiate that expansion. Being open minded, receptive to change, willing to learn and grow through every experience, and consciously appreciating your self during this cycle will make the journey much more acceptable. Surrender and acceptance of life *on life's terms* will increase your sense of adventure versus a sense of loss.*

You can trust that when you reach 40 you will see, feel and live life very differently. Many struggles will just fade away and your path will appear much clearer and more powerful if you allow the space in your life for change to express naturally. You will appreciate what you have invested in life to get here and the new experience of living that is now available to you.

*(Recommended reading: *The Power of Now*, by Eckhart Tolle and *Ask And It Is Given* by Esther and Jerry Hicks)

VULNERABILITY

When you fill in these empty emotional places, you will be able to *respond* to life instead of *react* to life. You react to life when someone's words, attitude, or behavior "reminds you" of your childhood. If the memory is one of lack, you react from that condition, defending or withdrawing to protect yourself because of your vulnerability. If it reminds you of pleasant memories, it brings you joy. Doing your "fill in" work gives you a greater sense of confidence, allowing your heart and mind to work together with greater harmony and empowers you to respond to the situation clearly by knowing who you are and how you really feel inside of you. You are responding to life from love and a sense of fullness rather than fear and a sense of emptiness.

DISCOVERIES

As you journey the Wheel of Life Cycles with a different set of eyes and allowing your heart to **feel** your reality and examine the conditions, you are "filling in" many empty places just by looking at them with your mind and consciously feeling them. Since everything is energy and information if you are just willing and able to be present, mentally, physically and emotionally, with what is going on in your life you can direct this energy and information in healthful creative ways in the moment it is happening. When you can do this, you truly can begin to live in the Present and create a life of conscious choice rather than one of reaction based on your past.

What you can feel you can heal.

What you can recognize you can direct.

DIRECTIVES

Over these 37½ - 40 years you have had the opportunity to feel many things, sometimes reacting and sometimes responding to them. Living your life by feeling your emotions and feeling safer with them provides you with the courage and desire to restructure your emotional foundation. Healing can only take place in the present moment, so no matter where or when the wounding occurred now is the time to heal it. You do not have to confront the catalyst of the past in order to heal your wounds today.

Life will continue to provide you with duplicate or similar situations to spark your feelings until you finally fill in your own emotional empty spaces and strengthen yourself, through love. acceptance and forgiveness of yourself and others. Then, lo and behold, you no longer need to call in those kinds of conditions or relationships anymore. You can celebrate this as a true graduation from an emotional empty space when your outer world reflects your inner progress. This is the true marriage, when what you feel and desire inside becomes a living demonstration in your daily life, that is truly integrity with your heart and soul.

As you create a conscious relationship with your emotions, you can consciously decide how you want to use this emotional power. Emotions are energy in motion and will follow the guidance of your conscious mind when freed from your past mental and emotional imprints. Feeling your emotions is the connection and directing them so the energy is freed to move through your body is the action. This is similar to the riverbank and the river. The riverbank is the structure that allows the river to flow to the ocean. The riverbank is not in charge of the flow, just providing a structure on the rivers journey.

Consciously being with your emotions in the moment of the experience is like the riverbank that supports the river of your emotional movement. Your sense of aliveness and well-being is dependent upon a healthy relationship with your emotions and their freedom to move in your life.

FOCUS

- **Willingness to change**

  Allow everything in your life to rearrange itself and be willing to stay strong and open to new life possibilities.

- **Receptive**

  Keep your heart and mind open to receive the blessings that come from expansion and change, even when it does not look or feel like a blessing.

- **Trust**

  To thine own self be true, which is your heart and soul's inner wisdom.

QUESTIONS AND GUIDELINES

1. The biggest empty space for me emotionally is. . .

2. How has this influenced my emotional foundation? my sense of comfort? my sense of safety?

3. List the emotions you feel safe and comfortable with.

4. List the emotions you feel unsafe and uncomfortable with.

5. Prioritize your list of uncomfortable emotions and begin to practice with one emotion per week creating a conscious relationship with this emotion so you can redirect this energy. Record what happens.

6. How has insecurity with your emotions influenced you in your relationships?

7. Do you want this to change?

8. How do you want your relating with others to be different?

40 to 42½ Years

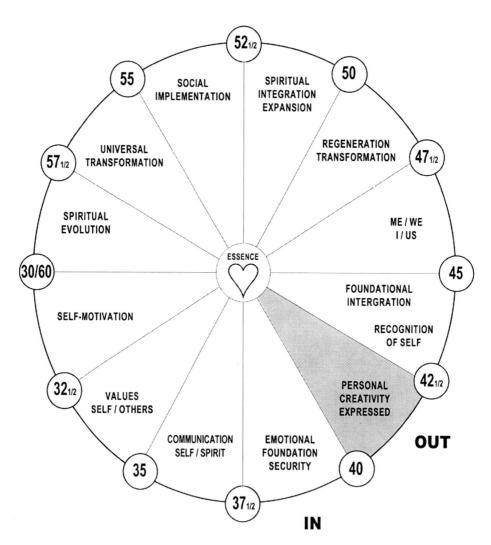

THEME

    Expression
    Creativity
    Aliveness

Chapter 20

Personal Creativity

POWER

CELEBRATE! You are just emerging from one of the most powerful and transformational life cycles, 37½ to 40, sometimes referred to as the "mid-life crisis". Do you feel like a butterfly rather than a caterpillar? Maybe you feel like the light is beginning to dawn and you are actually coming out of the tunnel of deep change. However you are registering this time in your life, something has changed. . . . trust yourself, *it is true,* even if your outer world "looks the same."

The more confident you are emotionally, the more you are ready to express your creativity. The big " emotional breath in" is over at 40 and you are really ready to "breathe out creativity" for the world to see; you are ready to create and deliver, feel your aliveness and enthusiasm and start spreading your wings and allowing your creativity to expand.

Now is the time, from 40 to 42½, for expanding your creative expression, and to discover and enjoy your talents and gifts and share them with others. Everyone is creative. Just because you are not an artist, actor, dancer, author, etc., does not mean you are not creative. Look at the areas in your life that bring you the most joy when you are doing them: What are these activities? These are your creative outlets, and whether you recognize it or not, your creative outlets are a blessing to others as well as yourself.

In the western culture we tend to focus all our attention on the blossom, forgetting we could not have a blossom without the rest of the plant. So if your creativity is not registered in your reality as a blossom, don't stop there, continue to be in appreciation of who you are and what you really love to do and do more of it. Everyone will benefit from your joy delivered no matter how you create your expression. *You are the blossom.*

VULNERABILITY

Your creative inner child is the heart and voice for your soul's wisdom, which is timeless, formless and ageless. Your creative inner child is continuously available to be adventuresome and creative in any way that your adult self will permit. Give yourself permission to look for new adventures during this cycle and try them out to see what happens. This cycle is about exploration, not necessarily implementation of a plan. If your passion awakens your creative power and takes hold of your life, directing you through your heart, listen and **go for it**. Otherwise, ride the multiple tides of creativity and you will be enriching your life experience so your innate desires can be expressed fully when the time is right.

DISCOVERIES

When you were 10 to 12½ years old, you may have been experimenting with many interests, seeking to find outlets that really satisfied you. What were your heart's desires at that age? Maybe you started something and dropped it or had to give it up and it is still of interest to you. Give yourself the opportunity to explore those desires now. The key in this cycle is that you are seeking an increased sense of aliveness. This feeling is not generated from outside of you and what you bring in. It is generated from inside out: what you are willing to express and demonstrate in your life that enhances and increases your sense of aliveness and joy. A dream is a wish your heart makes. . . .and now is the time to allow that dream to have life and aliveness through your creative expression.

DIRECTIVES

Anything that allows your joy to flow freely is a creative outlet and needs to be consciously nurtured, integrated into your life regularly and enjoyed immensely. Your joy is your soul power of renewal for you mentally, physically, and emotionally. Living your joy is one of the strongest supports you can provide for sustaining your immune system. Joy is the root of your aliveness and must have expression in order for you to feel and be alive. Joy is not a by-product of life. It is an innate, abiding expression of your heart and soul.

Creativity is your commitment to give life to the gifts that you were born with. Your gifts to life are eternally in safe keeping in your heart and soul, awaiting the curiosity of your mind to join with your heart and release your creativity. Being creative is the balancing factor of life. You breathe in, receiving life in many forms and experiences and you must also breathe out, giving back to the Universe your own special talents, skills and abilities. This is how the hologram of humanness is created and balance is maintained, breathe in, breathe out.

You have a contribution to make. Do not minimize your creativity because it does not have a label (artist, dancer etc) or look like anyone else's creativity. You are unique, Share your uniqueness with the world, that's why you are here on the planet. Nothing is impossible. Make the contribution that only you can make. You will feel so alive and the rest of us will feel so blessed. A great win/win for everyone.

Until one is committed, there is hesitancy,

the chance to draw back, always ineffectiveness.

Concerning acts of initiative (and creation) there is one elementary truth,

The ignorance of which kills countless ideas and splendid plans:

The moment one definitely commits oneself, then Providence moves, too.

All sorts of things occur to help one that would never otherwise have occurred.

A whole stream of events issues from the decision, raising in one's favor

All manner of unforeseen incidents and meetings and material assistance,

Which no man could have dreamed would come his way.

Whatever you can do,

Or dream you can, Begin it.

Boldness has genius, power and magic in it.

Begin it now!

Johan Wolfgang von Goethe

FOCUS

- **Listen**

  Have the courage to hear your deep heart's longing. This is where your passion and power reside for creating.

- **Trust**

  Trust your heart. Trust your desire. Trust your curiosity and spontaneity. Then take action on these truths.

- **Enjoy**

  Joy is the voice of your heart and soul in your daily life. If you are not enjoying your life or 'in joy' about life, your heart and soul do not have a voice; your creativity is the voice for your heart and soul.

QUESTIONS AND GUIDELINES

1. List three things that you love to do. Are you doing them in your life now?

2. If not, why not? (Notice the reasons you use to deny yourself joy.)

3. Do you recognize that your creative expression is essential for your mental, emotional, physical and spiritual health and well-being?

4. Create a plan that will incorporate your creative expressions in your life on a daily basis.

5. Do you have any resistance to doing this?

6. What are your excuses or habits you have created for denying or comprising your joy?

42½ to 45 Years

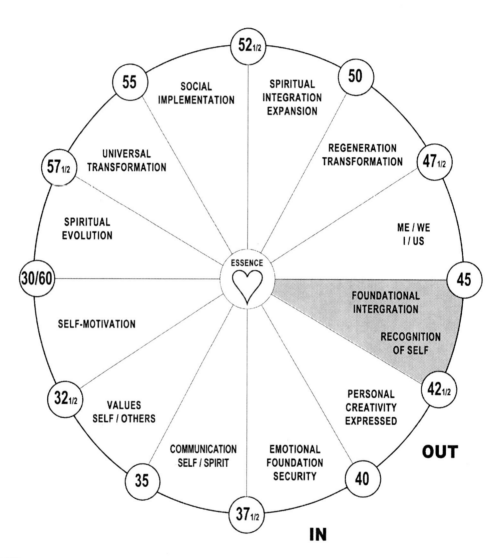

THEME

Integration
Stabilizing
Strengthening

Chapter 21

Integration

POWER

What has been happening in your life since you were 30 years old until this cycle at 42½ - 45? The life events that you have experienced during these last 12 years are creating a new foundation for you. This foundation is influenced by the first foundation you created from birth to 15 years old. This current foundation is overlaid on your life experiences that span from 30 to 45. These foundational years strengthen your inner world and inner awareness so as you expand into the world from 45 to 60, your sense of self-confidence and self-esteem is powerful and supportive for you.

Refer to the ages of 12½ to 15 when you were weaving your first foundation to be ready to meet the world as a young adult. What was happening for you then? Entering this cycle now at 42½ to 45, you have increased your life experiences. This time around, your buffet of life is bigger and provides more options for you to choose from. As you create your foundational structure this time around, it may become more apparent how all your life experiences are interwoven and your history is your present life and will become your future unless you are living from a renewed foundation of beliefs and behaviors. Your choices today determine where your life force will go tomorrow.

VULNERABILITY

During this cycle, there is such a strong inner drive to expand and make changes in your life. It may be a deep inner knowing and not articulated in your thinking as a "plan in life" so you could feel a sense of frustration or non-movement, even though you "know" something new is emerging. Because of the power of this cycle, there are usually many life changes that occur to accommodate your expansion in life. This can cause a sense of overwhelm especially if everything seems to come at once. It is important to enroll a support team so you can brainstorm with them personally and then include others who are professionals in their field who can help guide your changes and choices in your business, lifestyle, values, partnerships, parenting, etc.

Beyond this sense of frustration and any feeling of overwhelm is an opportunity for real adventure and excitement; there is so much happening in your life and creating a new world for you. Timing is everything so if you feel the changes are happening too fast or too slow, remember that the Universe is the master organizer and everything is orchestrated at some level for manifestation to be perfect and at exactly the right moment. Fasten your seat belt and enjoy your ride to expansion and greater discovery in life.

DISCOVERIES

An inventory of your life in the last 12 ½ to 15 years expands your awareness of how you are creating your personal foundation this time around and creating a new relationship with yourself, which influences your self-confidence throughout your life. Seeing yourself and your life experiences from your soul wisdom as well as linear thinking, allows a lot of your personal power and self worth to be reclaimed and become integrated into your daily life. This contributes to what society calls "being an adult" or "maturing". The bottom line is: when you have healed your life enough that you can make conscious choices that support and nurture you, rather than reactive choices that defend and protect you from your vulnerabilities, life takes on new dimensions of possibility and enjoyment. This is a worthy goal.

Recognizing that everything is energy and information supports you to live with a greater sense of ease and balance in a world of change. It does not take you 30 - 45 years to change your childhood conditions. It takes recognition. When you consciously direct the energy and information you discover, whatever the experience at any age, you begin to transform that condition. ***All transformation and healing can only take place in this*** *moment.* When you recognize your deep inner truth, the power of your truth transcends time and allows your heart and soul's inner wisdom to create your healing in a natural organic way. *We are born to be whole and healthy human beings expressing our soul's inner wisdom, each in our own unique way.*

DIRECTIVES

Review each cycle listed below by using a plus and a minus inventory.Using a piece of paper make two columns. Make one column, on the left a plus sign then list all the things you recogniz from each cycle that has added value to your life and is supportive for you. The minus column on the right represents all the things in your life that you are choosing to let go of or not include as part of your foundation in life, because they drain your energy and creativity.

30 - 32½   Attention, motivation, self-identity

32½ - 35   Values, quality in life and self-esteem

35 - 37½   Reconnection with Spirit, your truth and communication

37½ - 40   Home, family, foundation and emotional security

40 - 42½   Personal creativity expressed, aliveness, joy

42½ - 45   Foundational Integration, stability, balance

From each inventory, you can be clearer on what you have consciously acquired, or what you want to detach from at this time in your life so your current choices are based on what you want to use to stabilize and support your balance in life.

The keys for transforming your life are to be conscious of your choices, manage your thinking, and direct your focus in life with your mind, heart and soul in conscious partnership. What are you thinking? Power flows where your attention goes. When you are conscious of this, you can manage where your power goes, mentally, physically or emotionally, and begin to create a life that feels congruent with your heart and soul and is enhancing and fulfilling for you and others.

In reviewing your life with an expanded perception, you realize the internal Judge has got to go. You cannot have a Judge in residence, inside your head, and think you will **ever** get to see or experience your life differently. The internalized Judge has had years of practice telling you *what to do* and *what not to do*, enforcing the conditions you were subjected to and programmed by, throughout your life. Just because the Judge recognizes something it does not mean it is valuable or truthful for you in your life now. Discernment is the key. What is true for you today?

Retire the Judge. Invite this powerful energy to apply for the new position of the Observer, the one who discerns and reports new information to you so you can make heartfelt decisions, not just head-based decisions that come from life conditioning and fear-based reactions.

This shift in focus will provide you with more joy and ease than anything you can imagine, regenerating you on every level. A huge amount of your life force is wasted daily in conflict or compliance with your internal Judge. Freeing your mind to listen to the truth of your heart and soul is a rite of passage allowing your mind to be available to co-create, with excellence and uniqueness throughout your life.

FOCUS

- **Self-recognition**

  Now, more than ever, you are being asked by life to pay attention to who you are, how you feel, what do you want in life and accept what you discover.

- **Self-acceptance**

  With self-recognition, it is important to accept your uniqueness and life experiences and have confidence in yourself to strengthen your foundation and create the future you desire.

- **Appreciation**

Appreciation is a reward of self-acceptance. This allows you to see yourself just as you are and begin to appreciate the unique individualized qualities that are your gifts to share in life.

QUESTIONS AND GUIDELINES

1. What are the three most valuable strengths you have acquired since you were 30?

2. How are these strengths influencing the quality of your life now?

3. Is anything missing for you? If so, identify it and create a plan of action to begin to create and incorporate these qualities into your life now.

4. Measure your confidence and self-awareness today at 42½ - 45 compared to when you were 12½ - 15.

5. List three experiences from 30 to 45 that you recognize have transformed the way you live today.

6. What are your intentions and desire for the quality of life you want for the next 15 years?

45 to 47½ Years

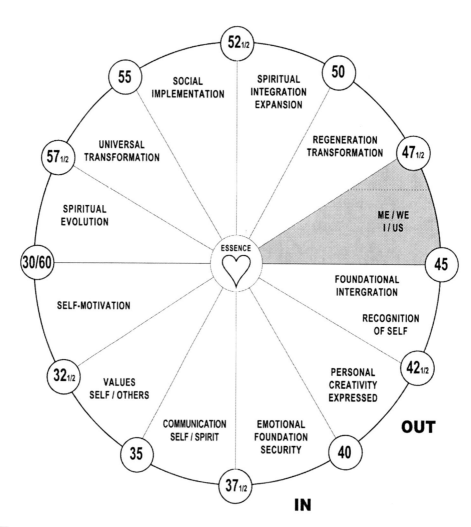

THEME

    Relating
    One on one
        Business
        Friendship
        Personal Partnerships

Chapter 22

Personal Relating

POWER

I believe that relating is the number one opportunity for growth for all of us on the planet. Our primary relationship needs to be with our body, then our emotions, our mind, the earth, the masculine/feminine energy, relating to others, family members, community, city, nation and the global family. With today's technology, our home planet is smaller and more closely knit than ever before. Everything is energy and information and we have always been influencing each other more than we understand or recognize and now relating through the Internet, we are discovering how intimately we share life and realities, in spite of our perceived differences.

Relating begins inside of you and me, before there is ever a "we". Relationship is a lifelong classroom and each person involved is both a teacher and a student. You magnetize the relating experiences in your life that will help you grow stronger and clearer, thus supporting you to live in partnership with your inner wisdom. *Relating continually bursts the bubble of isolation.* It really does matter how you think, act and behave because it influences all life. Many times in your life you may have heard or felt yourself say, "they make me angry, they hurt me, they. . . .something". This is a good indicator that you actually are interrelating with others and the differentiating factor is to recognize that no one can make you feel anything. Your emotions live and move only through your own body, they are your personal experience, no matter what activates the emotion.

The objective of any relationship classroom is to strengthen your conscious recognition of your inner values and truth in life, which comprise your foundation, so you can regain and maintain your personal balance and joyously share your life with another. The challenges you experience and grow through in partnership strengthen your authenticity and integrity, which in turn, influences your overall quality of life.

When you experience the illusion of separation from your heart and soul, you can feel disassociated from universal harmony and balance, which is innate in you and reflected in nature. Without conscious access to this template of divine order, you may lose your ability to know the importance of balance and cooperation with all life. Every aspect of your life suffers as a result of this sense of separation and can generate an eternal quest of seeking to return to your soul blueprint.

The physical body is constantly adjusting to the mental, emotional and nutritional influences that are out of harmony with nature. Live food carries the power of the earth that translates into nutrients to nourish our body. If you are out of balance in your body, this imbalance will be reflected in all your relationships, which assists you to become conscious of the imbalance so you can make conscious changes. The indigenous tribes have been offering guidance for centuries for the world to consciously awaken to nature's balance.

Without internal and external balance you cannot experience harmony and cooperation with another person or any form of life. If you do not feel an innate resonance with the balance and harmony of the earth, you are constantly trying to adjust your choices and lifestyle to create this condition emotionally. You may feel challenged because you have been trained to keep trying to make this connection with your head, *figure it out*, rather than follow your heart, which is always in resonance with the earth and your soul.

Are you clear about who you are in these issues:

- How you want to be seen, heard and recognized
- What motivates you
- Cooperation with others
- Being compassionate and caring,
- Honest and respectful lifestyle

Any of these missing qualities will continue to determine the lessons you will be "learning" during any relationship classroom.

The Universe is abundant and will continue to bring you another teacher/student dynamic, over and over, until you consciously address these lessons available in your relationships. When you learn how to manage your own needs and desires for yourself and not expect another to fill in your empty emotional spaces so you can feel whole, you will begin to experience that deep sense of inner peace. This is a lifetime experience of discovery and recovery… be patient with yourself in the process.

You teach the world how to treat and respond to you by the way you treat and respond to yourself. You are the magnet that attracts life to you by the way you think, feel and behave. Are you getting the attention you desire in the way you desire it? If not, look at the way you are treating yourself and determine what changes you want to make so getting attention will truly bring you your desired fulfillment. When you begin to change this inside model, then your outside experience will begin to change, and you can then create relationships that are more fulfilling and meaningful for you.

Gary Chapman has a book called the Five Love Languages that you may want to read. It offers simple and powerful ways to recognize your method of receiving attention and how to get your "love tank filled". Healthy relating requires a consistent and focused investment and recommitment by all parties involved. This is part of the adventure of being a human - we are always growing and changing in spite of our limitations.

DISCOVERIES

What a difference 30 years makes in perception and experience in life. When you entered the cycle of relating for the first time at the age of 15 (See Chapter 10) you were still in a state of comparative innocence in trying to get your needs met. Partnerships were a new experience, different than relating to your parents, caregivers or sibling.

Sometimes this could feel exciting and sometimes challenging or confusing. Most of your relating experiences were unconscious "experiments" and some worked and some didn't. This is how we learn – "hands on living," and as a result of your experiences you began to develop a "history" in relating to others and this "history" continues to influence your relating experiences to this day, at age 45.

If your head and heart feel conflicted and create a split inside of you, this is profoundly reflected outside of you, in all your relating experiences. Your heart is in resonance with the heartbeat of the earth, and thus the Universe, so you are always called "home" to your heart, no matter how your mind tries to deny your soul blueprint. Your heart is your place of balance and harmony as a human being, your "home" base.

No matter how frightening or challenging life may become, when in doubt, fear or confusion. . . .BREATHE consciously and slowly and focus on your heart - HOME BASE . Tap on your sternum (breast bone) at the heart level and say out loud over and over as you tap, "I deeply love and appreciate myself", until you feel your anxiety drop and your breath normalize. Then erase your forehead from the center out to the temples, doing this several times and saying out loud, "I release any energy that darkens my own Light." Drink a lot of water. These techniques will assist in reducing your emotional stress.

All the "stuff" that comes up, flies around, undermines, distorts and reconfigures relationships can help you begin to recognize and release imbalances inside of you that are influencing your relating experiences. *The truth shall set you free* and your truth is emerging constantly from your heart and soul seeking to influence your mind and daily choices. This can cause a lot of confusion until your heart, soul and mind get on the same page of life and there is a conscious commitment from your mind to honor and accept the divine plan that lives in your heart and soul; this creates a sense of oneness for you.

Relating on this planet, personally and collectively, is our number one classroom for humans and our relating experiences are dramatically changing every moment of our lives.

Whatever it takes to release you from the old constraints, limitations and beliefs about relating are appearing now so you can reconfigure your life and begin to create meaningful relationships. Relationship is not a destination. . . it is life in process every moment through the classroom of relating. Acceptance of your life, just as it feels and appears to you right now, is your rite of passage to change and freedom for your heart and soul.

If you recognize that your relationships are a passageway to your heart and soul's commitment, revealing unrecognized parts of you that feel empty, you can make new choices that will bring a greater sense of fulfillment for you. Through acceptance of your self you can grow stronger and clearer and learn from these experiences; then you do not have to continue to drag these lessons from one relationship to another, which means you have created another way to relate, from the inside out. You can actually create a long lasting, loving relationship by being willing to accept "what is" and commit to change your life so you can realize the joy and fulfillment you are seeking.

With this awareness you can consciously create relating in a new way based on what you have discovered about yourself in the last 30 years, since you were 15. You still have areas of innocence, innately in your heart and soul, and you also have acquired a lot of life experiences that are great partners for creating new relating skills.

What changes did you make from ages 30 to 32½ (See Chapter 16) that influenced the way you need and want attention? This is a foundational key for relating. If you are unclear or unconscious about getting attention, how could anyone relating to you be able to give you the healthy attention you are seeking?

Knowing what you do to get attention and whether this is healthy and balanced or covert and manipulative will directly influence your being able to relate to another and feel fulfilled, or not. Your life is about relating, so this is foundational for your clarity, fulfillment and joy as a human being.

DIRECTIVES

The key to balance in your life is to listen to the voice of your heart and soul. Integrate your life experiences, filter out the garbage of today or yesterday, accept every experience and allow life's blessings to emerge and become integrated into your reality. Be truthful with yourself and allow yourself to be very clear on what you really want in your life and what you do not want. Experience helps you discern these choices and this takes courage to tell yourself the truth, especially if it goes against the traditions or training of your youth. Deeply listen to the innocence in your heart and soul and accept what you truly desire for yourself in relating.

You relate everyday, on an energetic level, with everyone you contact. Your Presence in life makes a difference in every experience you have. You have the ability to create a healthy and balanced life that supports you and benefits the people you are relating to, consciously or unconsciously. Life is designed to be a win/win and we all have a lot of lessons to learn in order to create that as our lifestyle.

Whenever you are in a relating experience that feels "stuck," look for your fear or resistance somewhere in your life. Ask your self, "What am I afraid of? What am I resisting?" If you relate through fear or resistance, you may try to become invisible by withholding or withdrawing your energy from the situation. You may choose to position yourself defensively in order to protect your "fears and resistance," in an illusionary effort to feel safe. Energy cannot move easily when you are hiding or defending. Love cannot soothe or move when you are hiding or defending. Love and energy are synonymous.

Use this simple exercise to change those dynamics:

1. Consciously breathe, deeply and slowly

2. Command your mind to focus on your heart

3. Ask the fear or resistance to reveal itself to you (usually related to some sense of

loss or unfamiliar /unknown condition in your life)

4. Accept the fear or resistance without judgment.

5. Give the fear or resistance permission to transform into enthusiasm or acceptance or leave your mind/body.

6. Ask you heart, "What do you want me to do right now?"

7. When in doubt always choose love and acceptance for yourself and others.

Wherever there is stress, there is more fear or resistance than love or acceptance. Until you have the courage to release the fear and resistance and allow love and acceptance of the present condition, you will continue your defense and power struggles: you will not feel safe, loved or wanted. Be the one with the courage. Bring in the love and compassion and you can free yourself and then provide the space for other people to free themselves, if they choose to do so. Regardless, you will have moved yourself beyond the fear and resistance and closer to love and acceptance.

> *Being deeply loved by someone gives you strength,*
> *While loving someone deeply gives you courage.*
>
> Lao Tzu

FOCUS

• **Balance**

You must have some sense of balance in your own life before you can have any experience of balanced relationships in your life.

• **Trust**

Trust is an inside issue. You must first trust yourself, before you can ever practice trusting anyone else.

- **Respect**

Everyone is an individual and deserves to be respected and treated with loving-kindness. You do not know what is best for another person. It is a full time job to focus on what is best for you.

QUESTIONS AND GUIDELINES

1. List three areas of strength you have in relating to others.
2. List three areas of vulnerability you recognize in relating to others.
3. What do you need to know, or do, to change these areas of vulnerability into areas of strength and confidence for you?
4. Do you trust yourself emotionally to know what you want in relating to others?
5. If not, are you willing to increase your trust?
6. Do you have the courage to speak up and ask for what you want from another?
7. If not, are you ready to change this?

47½ to 50 Years

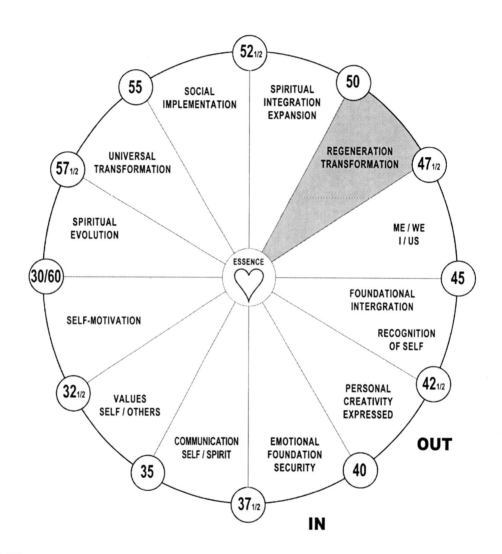

THEME

Self-empowerment
Emerging power
Personal and collective power

Chapter 23

Transformation

POWER

This is another one of those cycles where you learn to express yourself, claim your heart and soul wisdom and become more conscious of your influence as a global citizen by learning to recognize and manage your own power. From 17½ to 20 years old (See Chapter 11), life is like a rocket launching; all your power is moving with great force energizing the potential for the visions you can perceive. Now, 30 years later, you enter this cycle of transformation again, reinforced with your life experiences and your heart's desires to choose how you want to manage you energy/power and make even a greater contribution to life.

The collective unconscious is a neutral force field of power, directed by the intent and focus of the one who accesses it. This force field powered Hitler, Gandhi, and Mother Teresa. In the world of energy, we are all equal. We all have the ability to access this infinite power, determining its direction by the choices we make and the actions we take in our daily lives.

When you question life from your soul level commitment and recognize and direct your individual choices about how you use sex, money and power, your individual choices influence the collective consciousness. This is how you can co-create a future that can support our children's future for seven generations to come. Your life choices make a contribution today to tomorrow's balance and order for all life. Consciously or unconsciously, we are all shaping the future for our children with every choice we make and action we take.

VULNERABILITY

In this cycle you come face to face with your own power, recognized or denied. The quality of life on earth is influenced daily by the use or misuse of power on this planet displayed through the power of sex, money and greed. Notice that money and greed are human creations and our sexuality is a part of our divinity. What have we done in our human choices and behavior to tie these energies together in such harmful, irreverent ways? Each one of us is a part of the answer.

Your personal sense of values, quality of life, self-esteem and self-confidence are the underpinnings of your foundation in dealing with this collective power at this time in your life. This is the time to do an "inner inventory". The social, educational, cultural and religious conditioning you have experienced in life may have over-shadowed most of your soul purpose commitments. Have the courage to question how you were raised, what your family beliefs are, your religion, your educational training and how you were influenced in your community as your were growing up. How are these influences affecting your choices in life today?

DISCOVERIES

Your life is a vote. How you think, act and behave is using energy that demonstrates and enforces lifestyle patterns that are either life-enhancing or depreciating healthy quality living. How and where you spend your money is a vote for the attitude and behavior of those who create the product or service you purchase as well as those who manufacture and market it, including the retail outlet used to sell the product or service. Are you making conscious life-enhancing decisions how you spend your time, energy and money? Does your time, energy and money spent support life and living or death and dying?

To individuate and consecrate your power, through your heart and soul, you need to know your own truth and have the courage to live your truth. This is your soul commitment, to recognize and live your truth. There is no one else on the planet with your fingerprints, DNA or soul blueprint, if your do not fulfill your soul commitment you have no "stand in". Once your soul commitments become more recognizable to you, your innate desires will motivate you to create the necessary changes in your life to allow you to express your soul purpose.

DIRECTIVES

The choices you make during this cycle from 47½ to 50 years really make a difference for you and the collective transformation. Your conscious thinking (1/8) is not designed to manage Universal power. Your heart and soul are the innate director of this unlimited power. Now is the time to bring in your heart and soul (7/8) in conscious partnership with your mind (1/8) and ask meaningful questions of yourself about your relationship with your own sexuality, your use of money and your position with greed. Where are you? Where do you want to be with these energies? How do you want to invest your life and for what cause?

To create your inner inventory, use a piece of paper for each category: Values, Quality of Life, and Self-Esteem. Place the title at the top of the page, divide the page in half with a line down the center. On the left side of the line near the top of the page place a + (plus sign) and on the right side of the line near the top of the page place a - (minus sign). Plus stands for *what I want to increase in my personal life and on the planet*. Minus stands for *what I want to be reduced or released from my personal life and on the planet*. Then begin to record, under the plus and minus signs, your ideas, intentions and desires. Once you have done an inner inventory, you will consciously be able to assess your thinking and choices much more easily. All healing takes place from the inside out.

From this discovery, you can recognize what is missing for you, and how you want to invest your time/life. When you know what you believe and *where you are*, in your thinking, you can decide and more clearly direct *where you want to go*. This awareness provides inspiration and motivation for you to manifest your soul commitments. Enthusiasm (the God within) is derived from your soul and enhances your sense of aliveness and joy; this is the beginning of living your bliss.

FOCUS

- **Responsibility**

  Recognize your ability to respond to life rather than react to life's conditions. Be self-referencing in order to respond to life from your own truth.

- **Unity**

  For every action, there is a reaction. All life is interconnected. We are not isolated expressions of humanity. Your life and the choices you enact make a difference in this world.

- **Courage**

  Rely on your innate courage residing in your heart and soul to guide your choices and decisions in your life and to support your steps of action for change.

QUESTIONS AND GUIDELINES

1. What kind of relationship do you have with your sexuality?

2. Do you perceive your sexuality as a divine gift?

3. Are you satisfied and fulfilled with the way you "spend your sexuality"?

4. Is money your God?

5. Have you made money your security? Is it working?

6. Do you recognize your soul and human self as partners on the same team of life?

7. How does this affect your perceived personality and self-esteem?

8. How would your life change if you accept responsibility for your divinity?

9. Do you deeply love and appreciate yourself?

50 to 52½ Years

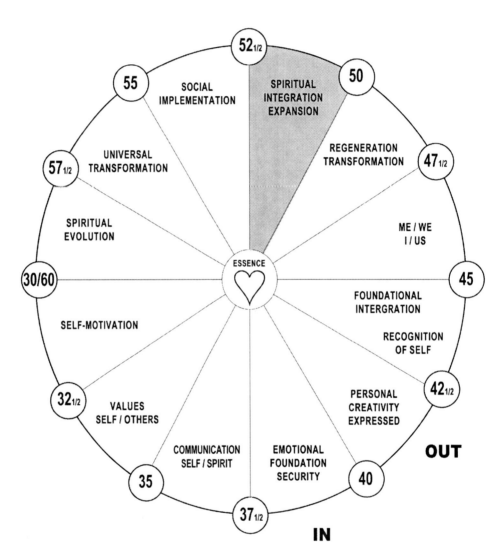

THEME

Inspiration
International awareness
Natural rhythm

Chapter 24

Inspiration

POWER

Your soul is a magnetic force field that entrains your heart and is a continuous call to higher consciousness. It is a call to Life: the power within the human body that magnetizes Life through the breath, everyday, over and over. Your soul calls you to live from your heart and acknowledge your higher consciousness and is especially strong and influential during this cycle, from 50 - 52½ years old.

You may discover that you are responding to philosophy, theology, new ideas, dreams, intuitions, imagination and all life in new and different ways. Some of this questing may be comfortable and some uncomfortable, that does not affect the quality of your adventure. When you were in this same cycle, from 20 to 22½, (See Chapter 12) your zest for life and new adventure was so powerful and full of enthusiasm you may have enrolled in many levels of thinking and exploration, including drugs. Your youth, lack of life experience and the quest for expansion and adventure were enough to motivate you to be open to many unknown possibilities. The call from your heart and soul is eternal and magnetizes you to new levels of consciousness no matter what your past has been.

As a child you naturally relate to life according to how you feel in the moment. Spontaneous living is a foundational aspect of childhood. The older you get the less spontaneous you become because you are trained that you are supposed to "grow up" and "behave yourself". Growing up doesn't mean giving up your joy or your visions. Joy is your eternal link to your innate aliveness. If you lose your sense of joy, your life force is diminishing with every breath. Growing up is a natural process of learning how to manage your energy, in ever-increasing ways; it does not require that you give up your joy and enthusiasm in life.

This cycle is calling you to your enthusiasm and spontaneity. You can renew and expand your aliveness if you really trust your deep inner knowing and have the courage to be adventuresome and explore beliefs, situations, relationships, and life opportunities in non-traditional options.

VULNERABILITY

An ordinary life just won't fill the bill any longer. You know there is something missing for you. Everyday of your life you are called to be in partnership with your heart and soul, and during this cycle, either you consciously put some focus in that direction or your soul will provide "classrooms of learning" where you can no longer avoid your truth. Your truth is the guiding Light upon your path of life and if you have relegated this power to silence or denial, your path is dimly lit and can appear unsafe and too small. This would definitely influence your sense of safety and enthusiasm for expansion in your life.

You may have had enough life experiences and situations that you liked or did not like, and you may have developed caution and skepticism as a result of those experiences, which could influence your desire to explore or expand your life for fear of loss or being hurt again. You can change yesterday's experiences by showing up today in a new way.

Even if your mind believes in separation, your life cannot stray far enough away from your soul to ever get lost. Separation is an illusion created by human thinking and it is an invalid principle in relationship to the Universe. If you feel lost, it is a feeling, it is an illusion based on your beliefs about separation and "buying the life appearances", rather than trusting your heart and soul. You can never be "lost" from your heart and soul because this is your primary relationship with all life. If you choose to ignore your innate desire to recognize your heart and soul then you can create the experience of "feeling lost" because your beliefs create a split reality, based on fear and denial of Universal principles.

DISCOVERIES

When you live in conflict between your mind and your heart and soul, this split will be reflected in your health, your attitude towards yourself and others and your inspiration for the future. This can occur if you build up enough shame, blame and judgment against yourself to feel unworthy to "come home" to your heart and soul. Your heart is "home base". Unity is innate; conflict is a human creation. Forgiveness of yourself and others is the key that opens the doorway of your heart to safely recognize unity with your soul and consciously live in Oneness, your natural state of being.

How many hours a day are you spending in a time schedule that feels restrictive and unnatural for you? Are you participating in personal or professional relationships that are diminishing for you? Imagine the joy of your childhood when you could be free to just explore life and wonder about the wonders of the Universe. This spontaneous part of you is still eager to have the freedom of exploration and adventure, matching your inner rhythm that motivates and excites your creativity, a foundation for your natural rhythm. Included with this, is the power of curiosity. Curiosity and innocence are a lifeline to your inner creative child. Be excited when you can say, " I do not know." This reveals a release of your conscious mind to "always have to know" which allows universal consciousness to bring in new information open to unlimited possibilities.

DIRECTIVES

Be willing to open your mind to go beyond your beliefs--the man-made laws, institutions, government, legal, social and educational systems--and listen with your heart and soul calling you to a greater awareness of the divine gift of life and your part in it. Your personal truth creates your path of life and reality that you live with.

This is such an important time to really question:

- What are your beliefs about life?
- How did you learn these beliefs?
- Does your heart accept these beliefs?

Questioning your beliefs is an invitation for your inner truth to emerge. Give yourself permission to consciously have a relationship with your inner truth. Your heart and soul can reveal true values to your consciousness to recognize what beliefs and desires are motivating you.. Power flows where your focus goes, and conscious recognition and choices can create a new relationship with all life. You can begin to feel excited about change even when it feels frightening or challenging.

Your soul is your innocence, the true communion with all life, free of human distortions. Innocence is not weakness; it is energy of pureness that provides a direct avenue to the power of the Divine. In your innocence you are open and available to the power of your soul and divine guidance. That pureness of spirit, curiosity, and the joy of aliveness are seeking expression through you right now. Go For It!!

FOCUS

- **Truth**

   Your innate Self recognizes the wisdom of the ages and is seeking an expression through your life now.

- **Receptivity**

   Nothing new is born from constriction. Open your heart and mind to receive the universal awareness that lives within you.

- **Joy**

   Joy is an abiding experience in your heart and soul and constantly seeks expression in your life. Accept this gift of life now.

QUESTIONS AND GUIDELINES

1. Do you recognize your intuition/inner voice?

2. Are you listening to your intuition/inner voice?

3. Do you trust this divine power?

4. Do you trust your ability to hear your intuition/ inner voice clearly?

5. What is the worst thing that could happen to you if you listen and follow your intuition/inner voice?

6. What is the best thing that could happen to you if you listen and follow your intuition/inner voice?

7. In taking steps of action based on what your intuition/ inner voice is asking you to do, rate your level of courage, from 1 to 10 with 10 being the most courageous.

8. Do you have fears about taking these steps of action?

9. What is the cost in your life if you do not listen and follow your intuition/inner voice?

52½ to 55 Years

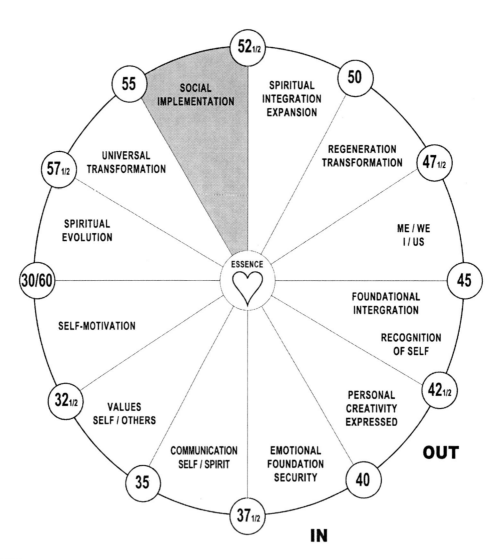

THEME

Career/ Profession
How you are seen in the world
Outlet for your creativity

Chapter 25

Public Identity

POWER

How do you want to be seen in the world? This is a big question in life and particularly at this age. In the first journey through your life cycles, at age 22½ to 25, (See Chapter 13) your enthusiasm opened many doors for work, career, profession, vocation . . . . whatever you were seeking at that time. This was your first time through this cycle and everything was an adventure and could at least start out as exciting and interesting. It has now been 30 years since you were in this cycle and you have experienced a lot of life and your sense of what is inviting and exciting has dramatically changed. Some of the influence in this cycle comes as a result of your life assessments and changing your belief systems in the last 30 years.

Your relationship with authority is different now since you are in a position, by age alone, to be considered a "wise one". In an indigenous culture, the elders are the wisdom keepers and highly revered for their knowledge of life, as well as their ability to draw on their ancestors' wisdom--those who have gone on before them. In a consumer-based culture, the older you get the more disposable you become. You do not have to allow this consciousness to create your reality unless you subscribe and invest in these beliefs. By this cycle, the consumer values that are based on the "outside" world don't hold the same power of attraction or motivation for you, so your choices for work and compensation are more discriminating.

You change your world by changing your values and your relating criteria. When you relate to yourself as a soul the consumer value system is not as influential in your life as it has been. This alone sets you apart, giving you a new sense of autonomy and potential. If your identity and value are not dictated by an illusionary, arbitrary value system, you can begin to listen to your soul and hear the truth of who you are and what you are doing on this planet. From this vantage point you then make clear decisions on how you want to be seen, heard and recognized with choices that are congruent with your true values of life.

VULNERABILITY

This cycle is influenced by your emotional foundation developed from 7½ to 10 (See Chapter 7) and from 37½ to 40 (See Chapter 19). If your emotional foundation still has empty, vulnerable spaces, this can show up in this cycle through insecurities, defensive behaviors, procrastination, sabotage; some of the things we do when we feel unsafe and lack confidence in ourselves. These behaviors could show up anywhere in your life and strongly in your career or professional life.

Pay attention to these behaviors and feelings that you may not like. They are precious messengers of latent power seeking release to new ways of living. If you recognize these experiences as messengers notifying you of the vulnerabilities in your emotional foundation, you can heal these conditions and redirect this power in a positive way. *What you can feel you can heal. What you can recognize you can redirect.*

DISCOVERIES

There is no way after the changes in your awareness field in the cycle from 50 - 52½ that you can enter this cycle from 52½ to 55 and have the same outlook in life that you had 30 years ago. Your level of discernment, consciousness, and quality determines where and how you want to invest your life at this time. It is extremely important for you to determine how you spend your time, which you now recognize is your life, and what kind of investment is returning to you and what is the quality of that return. Everything is energy and information and the choices you make determine your investment and return--the natural law of the Universe: for every action there is a reaction.

In this cycle particularly, you really get to recognize how all aspects of your life influence the choices and direction of today and your future. Whatever has been unconscious, denied, undiscovered or unrecognized, will emerge at some point in your life to be received, healed and redirected. That is the power of your soul, always calling your experience of life to the highest level of expression. This cycle magnifies all these hidden areas and requests integration between your head and heart so unity can emerge.

DIRECTIVES

You are the director, producer and star in your life movie, similar to the movie industry. In America there are many original movies that are being "re-made" for today's audiences, not at all dissimilar to how your "life movie," is constantly being "re-made, updated."

This cycle is your personal chance to redirect and recast the original version of your work/public life and actively participate as the director until you get the movie that you desire, what you truly envision for your life. Rearrange your beliefs, attitudes and behaviors according to your true value system and you have the foundation to remake your life movie from the inside out. Power flows where your focus goes. Whatever your script in life has been, it is always available for revision and renewal. The clearer you are on your intended life, the closer you can come to producing your vision.

FOCUS

- **Listen to your heart**

  If you do not listen to your heart, no matter what you do or how successful you appear you will not feel fulfilled, because your heart's desires will be missing.

- **Self-reference**

  You have a commitment to bring your special and unique gift to life, and you cannot do that if you do not honor your inner wisdom and guidance.

- **Trust yourself**

  Your link to life is through your heart and soul. If you don't trust yourself and this primary relationship, all other life experiences will be tainted with your lack of trust in yourself.

QUESTIONS AND GUIDELINES

1. What is your intended goal for this 2½-year cycle at this time in your life?

2. How are you different now than you were 30 years ago when you were 22½ - 25?

3. List three things in life that you consider necessary to create a quality life for yourself.

4. List three qualities that are essential for you to be willing to invest your time and energy in, in order to receive money.

5. How are you "spending" your energy and consciousness in life?

6. Are you getting the return from life that you want and deserve?

7. If not, why not?

55 to 57½ Years

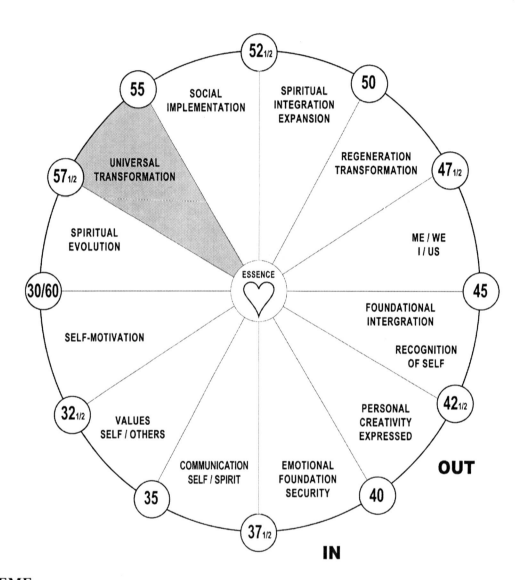

THEME

Humanitarian needs
Global family awareness
Transformation

186

Chapter 26

Universal Awareness

POWER

Expansion is aliveness. Aliveness is expansion. Everything in your life emerges from the inside out, seeking expression and calling for a bigger view of life, bigger stage, a bigger movie screen for your life experiences. The movie you are in right now began opening when you were in this cycle from 25 to 27½ (Chapter 14). During this cycle at 55 - 57½, your focus expands on humanitarian needs of the global family. You now have 30 years of experience to draw on now for potential global solutions. We are all a part of the global family living on this home planet. We are an interdependent species and our lives depend on the Earth and many forms of life for sustenance. All life is encoded energy and interconnected; every choice and action we make influences collective unity and the future for our children. During this cycle your focus is attracted to the bigger picture of life and how you can begin to consciously work together as part of a team for global transformation. Your inner desire is a driving force so you can make a difference in life.

VULNERABILITY

The model for all life is a family model; every species has some "source" or "parenting aspect" that co-creates life and influences the life force in each species. If we look at the conditions in life right now we can see the distress of the global family reflecting the distress of the individual and personal family. As you come to new levels of awareness and participation with your soul commitments you will feel a greater sense of fulfillment and purpose in your own life, inclusind your human needs as well.

Accepting your own personal creative expression plays a big part in how valuable you feel as part of the global family. Review Chapters 8 and 20 to see how that time period in your life influences your sense of fulfillment and natural creativity during this cycle. You may discover that in your family of origin you did not feel recognized for your creativity and your personal values and desires were not validated. As you acknowledge and share your ideas, values, desires and creativity with your community, organizations, and your personal and global family, you may experience a whole new sense of recognition and validation for who you are and what your gifts and talents are. Everyone is unique. Your gifts to life are uniquely your own. These gifts have no life until you express and share them with others. Until you give your creativity life, through your unique expression, it is simply an idea, a vision, or a possibility.

DISCOVERIES

This cycle calls you to really look at what it means to consciously be a part of the global family and what are your commitments to family at this level. In America, particularly, this is not a common thought. Since everything is energy and encoded information,we are energetically connected to all life. With the advancement of technology, the Internet and the World Wide Web, the global family is instantly connected in ways we may never have known before. With this technologically we are becoming more familiar with the energy network that connects all life and what influence we as humans have on the balance in life by the choices we make every day. This is such a wonderful time to consciously begin to make choices that will insure the future for our children in safety and peace. (See *The World Is Flat* by Thomas Friedman.)

A quantum leap in consciousness takes place when a focused group of people come together with clear intention. If the human family consciously begins to live as a global family working together for a healthy, loving safe environment for all life, we will experience "miracles"; changes that occur beyond our ordinary expectations and yet are the ordinary in universal consciousness.

Your recognition in this cycle, of your true potential to influence the world instills new options and possibilities for sharing your soul purpose in life. Now is the time to *be* all that your heart desires.

DIRECTIVES

When we realize that our human life has a dependency on this earth, the sooner we can begin to consciously live as a global family and use our creativity to heal ourselves and share this with all life on this beloved planet. Our unconscious choices created these problems and within our heart and soul are the solutions, if we will honorthe Earth and receive the guidance that has sustained and transformed all life throughout time.

Your level of comfort with your personal creative gifts and your level of confidence in sharing them with others will determine the scope of your expression in your life right now. There is no limit to your possibilities unless you create limits. The world is your playground and the needs of humanity are unending. Somewhere, life is magnetizing you to be exactly who you are and to share what you desire to give to the world. Are you open to the call from your heart and soul? This call may come to you in ordinary ways: through your imagination, the newspaper, the TV, the radio, a neighbor, your child, the grocery store clerk, the angry relative or your own dreams and intuition. Your heart and soul are always calling you to your greatest expression and fulfillment, and this innate power is infinite and available in your life every day wherever you go. Make sure you are consciously available by allowing you mind to listen to the inner wisdom. You promised yourself that you would be of service in this lifetime. **Now** is the time.

I do not know what path in life you will take, but I do know this:

If on that path you do not find a way to serve,

You will never be happy.

Albert Schweitzer

FOCUS

- **Collective awareness**

  You are interconnected with all life; we all share the same breath. Be conscious of your choices and the long-range influences for you personally and collectively.

- **Personal responsibility**

  Do not take life personally but be personally responsible for your life and your choices.

- **You are a gift**

  When you recognize and claim your innate abilities and purpose on this planet, you can consciously make your contribution to humanity, fulfilling your soul purpose.

QUESTIONS AND GUIDELINES

1. List 3 things your heart has desired and wanted to do throughout your life.

2. What action do you need to take to make these desires a reality?

3. What are your gifts you have to share with the global family?

4. In the global family, list 3 needs that you recognize are common to all people?

5. Do you consider all races equal?

6. Where did you learn to make your assessment of this value?

7. Is this your truth?

8. What does "humanitarian needs" mean to you?

9. What does "brotherhood systems" mean to you?

57½ to 60-years

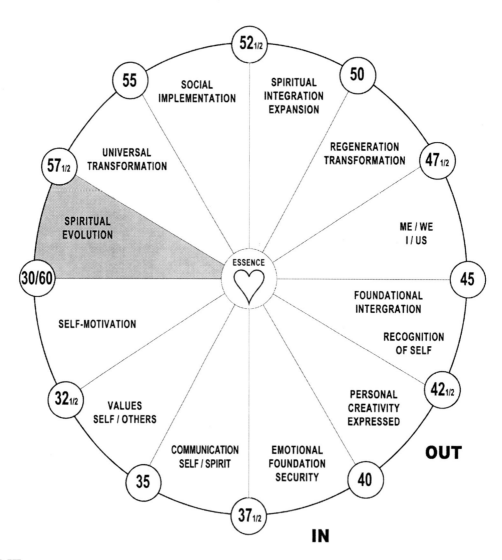

THEME

Inner renewal
Spiritual regeneration
Personal inventory

Chapter 27

Spiritual Foundation

POWER

During this cycle you re-enter the womb of Spirit, preparing to give yourself a new life at age 60. This is the second time you have entered the womb of Spirit to co-create a new life for yourself, first at 27½ to 30 and now 57½ to 60. In the first cycle at 27½, you reviewed your life from birth, and consciously or unconsciously, chose the lifestyle that you carried forward at age 30. The last 30 years are now here for review: what lifestyle do you want to create for yourself this time as a foundation for the next 30 years?

You do not have to be born again as an infant; you are reborn in the same body when you change your relationship with your mind and your heart and soul. Life is a renewal process: your body renews your cells daily, the earth continuously renews life, and your breath renews your commitment to be alive. When your conscious mind is cooperatively in relationship with your heart and soul, you will have new life experiences. During this cycle you are embraced by your soul and enfolded by the divine plan as you renew your commitment to love, life and creation.

Love is the law, and partnership on every level of life is the vehicle for humanity.

VULNERABILITY

Since you are preparing for a rebirth, it is very natural during this cycle to feel drawn to more inward activities. You may feel better in smaller gatherings than larger groups, and more intimate settings may feel more comforting for you. You may have the desire to meditate, read, contemplate, walk and have more quiet time for yourself; this is very natural, appropriate and supportive for this cycle in your life.

193

We are so accustomed to viewing "surrender" as a loss that you could feel fearful about letting go of your lifestyle, as you have known it. If the pitcher is full of orange juice, you can't put water in it until you empty the pitcher. The space you are creating is giving you room for a new lifestyle to emerge. It is natural to feel nervous or fearful when you make changes, big or small. Your conscious mind is distressed by conditions in life that are unknown or unfamiliar. Just be patient and calm and reassure your mind that your heart-driven choices are healthy and in your highest interest.

If you experience feeling lost as you consciously reunite with your heart and soul, this is a symptom of remembering your soul purpose and commitments, which causes the mental illusion of separation to begin to fade. Home base is your heart and soul and when you feel this truth "inside" you it becomes the reality you demonstrate "outside" through the partnership with your conscious mind. The law of grace always provides another chance to make another choice. The sun comes up every day. You have a chance to choose again, no matter what your choices may have created. You can live differently by choosing life in cooperation with your heart and soul awareness.

DISCOVERIES

The energy of this cycle can feel very mixed. Many times during this cycle you are letting go of ideas, life conditions, and sometimes relationships and work. You may experience relief and excitement as well as anxiety or a sense of non-direction. Be present with each day, each feeling. My grandma used to tell me, "This too shall pass". There were many times in my life where I felt that was just 'grandma's saying' and yet, as life changes, I have experienced that everything really does pass on to the next experience and expression in life.

In preparing for a new life, it is as though you are creating a new movie, without a full script or cast of characters. Time will fill in the blanks, so patience with your self and life is very supportive right now. An inner process never "fits" with our mind's expectations. Surrendering to the inner timing in this cycle will bring you greater comfort.

Taking an inventory of your life and assessing what is important to you and what you want to include in the next 30 years of your life increases your sense of confidence in yourself and your future. You may feel unclear in more areas of your life than you usually do. This is natural for this cycle. Being in the spiritual womb brings your focus of life inward since you are examining and questioning your life up to this time so you can make new decisions for your future. Timing is everything so remember you are in this cycle for 2½ years; there is no rush, just stay conscious of your choices and intentions.

Since this cycle is so immersed in your inner wisdom, your mental clarity and decision-making process may feel foggy and unclear at times. This too is natural for the cycle you are in. Your creativity emerges through the receptive field of imagination and intuition. It is not a linear process. Receptivity is an inner experience, so you may feel more confusion than you usually do. Your outer experience is being influenced by your inner truth from your heart and soul, preparing an expanded foundation for the next 30 years of your life. If you already have a conscious partnership with your mind, heart and soul then this expanding awareness at this time may bring you a sense of comfort and release. If this is a new experience for your mind, heart and soul to consciously work together, you could feel challenged and insecure in this cycle, even though it is the gateway to your inner awareness; it is still a time of major change.

Allow your trust and faith in yourself to increase by allowing time for you to adjust to listening deeply to your heart and soul as an authentic voice in partnership with your mind. You may notice that the ease in your life increases and you have less stress than when your mind was under the illusion "it was in charge" and didn't listen to your heart and soul's vote in your life. Celebrate, another illusion bites the dust.

DIRECTIVES

Give yourself permission to return to the pureness of your heart and soul. Renew your curiosity in life so you are open to change and make changes consciously motivated through joy rather than unconsciously through struggle and pain. The more you are willing to surrender old ways of living and thinking and take a risk with the potentials of life, the easier your new life emerges. Don't you believe the story that "you are too old!"

You are alive, breathing, walking, talking. . . .keep creating new life, consciously.

Life is an ever-renewing experience.

When you were born, even though you were created to walk, you were not born walking. When it was time for you to walk, you practiced over and over until you accomplished it. In this rebirth, you *can* walk, and the changes you will be making will need practice, the same way you learned to walk, so start with baby steps in the changes and be patient with yourself. There is no need to scare yourself to death by leaping off tall buildings while you are learning a new way of living in the world; to walk and talk with your heart and soul again. Make choices that are reasonable for your level of experience and trust in this renewed partnership with your heart and soul to safely guide you to new levels of expression and experience, and give yourself permission to take your time in renewing this partnership. Abiding joy is the gateway to your soul. Let this be your intended destination.

Since love grows within you, so beauty grows.
For love is the beauty of the soul.

St. Augustine

FOCUS

• **Listen**

Now more than ever, be respectful of your inner guidance, your intuition and your heart's longing. You have waited many years to be in this soul partnership.

• **Be willing to "let go"**

No matter how you have lived your life before today, be willing to open your mind to new ways of Being in the world.

• **Trust you**

Who is your constant companion on this journey of life? YOU!!! Respect this precious relationship and give priority to your heart and soul. Now is the time.

QUESTIONS AND GUIDELINES

1. Do you believe you can renew your life by consciously re-uniting with your heart and soul?

2. How will this affect your life now?

3. What is your intention for your life for the next 30 years?

4. Will you feel strengthened if you surrender your beliefs to the power of your heart and soul?

5. How is your life different in this cycle now than it was 30 years ago?

6. What do you perceive as the benefits of your heart and soul being in partnership with your conscious mind for the rest of your life?

WHEEL OF LIFE

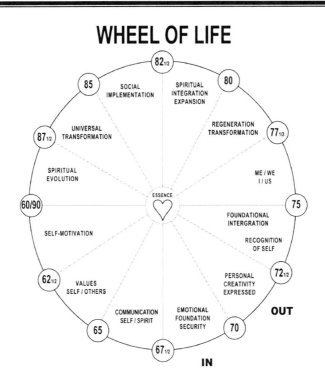

60 to 90 years

Spiritual - you have had 60-years of experience in this life school and chances are, nothing appears the same as it did when you were 30 years old. Many desires and passions of life that were motivating forces for you from 30 - 60 do not seem to have the same impact during this cycle. Your perception of life may have changed dramatically, depending on your ability to trust yourself and the universe you live in. During this cycle the focus is to return to your primary relationship with your heart and soul to experience the beauty, passion, power and wisdom of seeing life from the "big picture", the attributes that constitute quality living and what is truly enduring.

60 to 62½ Years

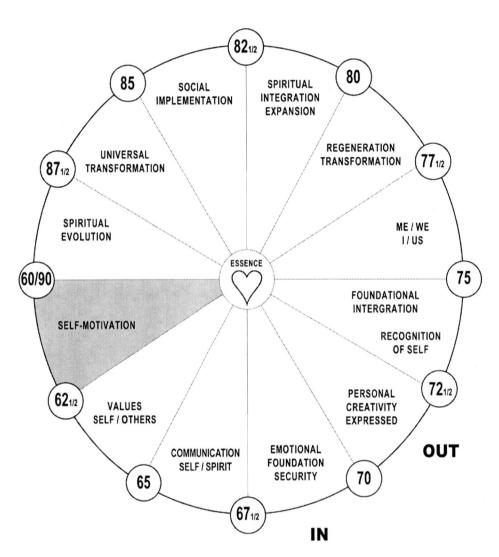

THEME

New identity
Personal motivation
New direction in life

Chapter 28

Attention and Motivation

POWER

Remember a song Frank Sinatra used to sing that said, "love, like youth, is wasted on the young"? Until you reach the age of an elder, those words are either offensive or you simply ignore them. When you reach the 60-year cycle, you hear those words from a deep place of appreciation that reminds you of all that you have experienced, felt, and created in your life since you were young. Only now can you see and feel the depth and breadth of many of those experiences because your vantage point is expanded and elevated through your own life experience and awareness.

One of the gifts this 60-year cycle brings is that you carry a deeper commitment from within yourself to be present in your daily life, to see and feel fully what your life is all about as it is happening. You may have missed this experience in your previous years because so much was happening on a daily basis that it was really challenging, and sometimes distracting and overwhelming, to just meet the experiences and conditions of life and maintain your balance, let alone feel truly present. This is one of the reasons that being a grandparent is so precious. You actually have time to enjoy the wonder of a child growing and changing daily.

VULNERABILITY

You do not have to change "who" you are for anybody. Most all of your life you may have been trying to satisfy others, seeking their approval, wanting to feel loved or at least get the attention that you desired. As you reclaimed your inner partnership with your mind, heart and soul during the cycle of 57½ - 60, your values changed. You discover that you do not have to change for others to love you; you now change for yourself. This allows you to let go of the need to be "outer" referenced or validated by someone or something outside of you to determine your value. Your deep inner wisdom awaits expression through your being "inner" referenced: trusting your heart and soul and recognizing you are indeed a wise elder, with wisdom to share.

When you release the outer-referenced perception of life, your inner movie begins to emerge and you will see and discover unknown parts of your self and ways that you were living, and not recognizing, because the "outer value system" was shaping your reality. Your world will never be the same from an inner-referenced value system. This assures you that the next 30 years can be a renewal of your life, a great new adventure.

DISCOVERIES

Sixty is a rebirth, a new beginning of life for you for the next 30 years. Don't get caught in the collective consciousness of "retiring," as if you are being put out to pasture. Consciously "retire" from the conditions and restrictions employment or any other lifestyle may have demanded from you and recognize that this is a *new life*, because you are retiring the old life. You have the ability and the experience to be clearer than you have ever been to create a life that is truly designed from your heart's desires. Being alive, living consciously and fully experiencing each moment as much as you possibly can enriches your life tremendously and the lives of those around you.

Attention is a primal need and must be honored as a foundational aspect to create balanced living. If you live an inner-referenced value system, based on your heart and soul expressing through your innate wisdom, your desires for attention are dramatically altered, which influences your lifestyle, friendships and relationships you have created in your life.

Since you were born, this is the third time you have been in this particular cycle, which is focused on your identity. Your identity is based on your perception of how you see yourself and how you want to be seen, heard and recognized by others. What do you feel you have to do to get attention? The natural stages of developing your identity are influenced each time you are in this specific cycle.

- The first time, from birth to 2½ years old, was creating your foundation for survival, done on a subjective primal level. The methods you developed in this cycle to satisfy your need for attention were survival based. Without physical attention, you were completely helpless to meet your primary needs. This anchors in the reality that as a human being, attention is essential, and throughout your life you will do whatever is necessary to get attention.

- The second time, from 30 to 32½, you were re-creating the identity that you would begin to use for your foundation to express who you are in the next 30 years. There is a natural progression of emerging consciousness in each cycle during this 30-year cycle, so every 2½ years you were reviewing and renewing your life in all the areas of your foundation. Some changes were subtle and some very obvious. No matter how the change occurred, it always does.

- The third time, from 60 - 62½, is recognizing and claiming your spiritual identity that you will use consciously sharing your wisdom and gifts with others for the rest of your life. This is the cycle of Being the wisdom. You do not have to study to accomplish this, or make it a goal or destination. Your inner wisdom will emerge naturally if you consciously live in partnership with your mind, heart and soul and allow your innate wisdom to be expressed.

Small movies of life seem to create Big problems. Big movies of life seem to create smaller problems. Everything is relative to your perception of reality. If you make your world small by living only in your linear mind, then any problem that arises will seem Big, because your mind is the one assigned to 'figure out what to do". If you make your world big by living from your deep inner knowing, then you have a team - mind, heart and soul, to assist resolving your problems. If you want your world bigger, give yourself permission to open up your mind and look at life differently and create your reality, beliefs, actions, and associations in alignment with your heart and soul. Everyday, life will present you with new choices for a different lifestyle.

DIRECTIVES

Now is the time to review and change your method of getting attention and allow your personal desires and wisdom to receive the attention you are truly seeking. It is safe, and timely, to surrender the method of getting attention that was based on an outer referenced value system of consumer consciousness.

Spirit lives through your heart and soul. Your inner wisdom doesn't just happen overnight or when you turn 60. You were born with this wisdom and have been using it and sharing it, throughout your life, in many ways you probably don't even recognize. Timing is everything so the deep inner knowing that you have held close to your heart, and consciously or unconsciously may have been yearning to share and explore with others, can now become a reality. You are the dream and the dreamer waking up to a new world now.

Try something you have *never* done before and see what happens to your life. Renew your curiosity and give yourself permission to experience life as the greatest adventure you have ever been on and you have a new way of living in this life, by the choices you make today. This is beginning of the rest of your life and it is never too late to have a happy childhood and let your magnificence shine.

FOCUS

- **Personal desire**

  Many years of your life have been spent focusing outside of yourself, on others. What is it that you really want in life for yourself? It is time to be inner motivated by your personal desires that honor your inner wisdom.

- **Personal intention**

  When you are clear on what you want, then focus on the steps of action you intend to take in order to satisfy your personal desires.

- **Personal satisfaction**

  How do you want to feel when your desires are met? Have you ever felt this way before? If so, you know what that feels like; if not, you are in for a wonderful new experience that you are consciously creating for yourself. Bravo!

GUIDELINES AND QUESTIONS

1. Are you getting the attention you truly desire or behaving from old habits and still feeling unfulfilled?

2. What would your life be like if you were not "arranging" it for someone's approval?

3. Who are you really?

4. Why are you on this planet?

5. What are the qualities of the person you 'want to be' in your life at this time?

6. Do you appreciate the wisdom you have acquired from your life experiences?

7. Are you willing to assume your role as a mentor in society and share your wisdom?

62½ to 65 Years

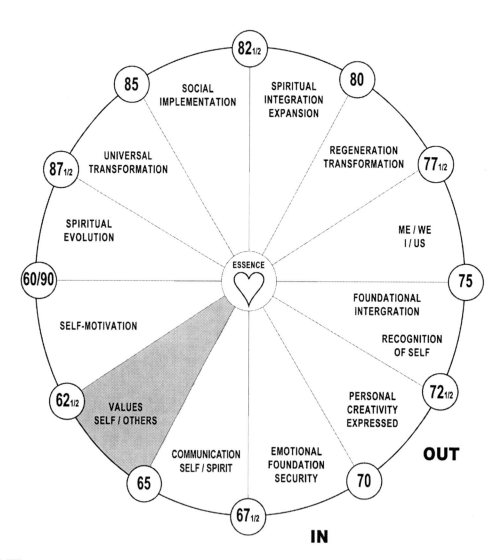

THEME

>Personal values
>Quality of lifestyle
>Personal comforts

Chapter 29

Values

POWER

Your view of life and your personal values are completely different than they were in the previous cycles when you were 2½ - 5 years old or 32½ - 35. This is a more introspective experience this time around in this cycle. You are generating a more intimate relationship with your inner values and qualities that you have chosen to have in your personal life. Even though you have been in this cycle two times before and it may feel familiar this time around is a new experience because your life is not the same as it was 30 or 60-years ago. Recognizing that your life is "different" now defines your starting point for generating the values and qualities in life that you prefer. You are getting clear enough to know what you really want and what is deeply satisfying to your mind and also your heart and soul.

You may discover that you are not so "outer-driven" by time schedules and social commitments in the same way that you may have been for years. You actually have more quality time to be still and listen to your heart and soul, which can become a significant voice in your life now.

The key for your comfort during this cycle is to really access your true values in life, *what makes your heart sing*, and let those values guide your choices in life. When you listen to your inner wisdom, then you begin to create your lifestyle by trusting your partnership between your mind and your heart and soul. When you align with your personal truth and your inner values, you are choosing wholeness rather than separation in your life and this will guide the use of your energy for renewal and regeneration.

VULNERABILITY

From 62½ - 65, every value you have ever thought was important will be up for review. Sorting through your values, strengthening your self-esteem and self-confidence through your heart and soul will alter your quality of life and establishe a value based foundation congruent with your inner desires. At this age, the grip of consumer consciousness does not have the same influence on your thinking, allowing you to begin to develop a foundation that has values and a lifestyle that repflects what you really want in life. You are no longer a slave of the two-faced god: time and money, at least not in the same way.

Whether you are measuring the relationships you have, the way you use your creativity and sexuality, the conditions on the planet, or the food you eat, everything in your life is up for renewal. Allowing yourself to go through this passageway of renewal with the deepest faith in your soul's guidance and listening to your heart will provide a gentle transformation. You can blossom naturally, free of pain and drama. Crisis is not a criteria for growth.

DISCOVERIES

As children growing up, one of the aspects of discovery is asking questions, which may include questioning the authority figures in our life. These qualities are important from 60 - 90 as well. Questioning life, on every level, takes you out of the illusion of your beliefs and allows you to see and release any illusions more easily and so you can become more authentic with *your* true values in life. This is how you "come home" to your heart- ask questions, drop your illusions and recognize what is your personal truth in life.

During this cycle, it is important for you to have an active Observer Self that looks at everything in your life as energy and information, and how this energy and information is flowing, or not. The Observer Self has the task of gathering information and providing additional options to support making new decisions on how you want to "spend your energy": what quality of life you want to create for yourself and your loved ones at this time. By assessing the quality of your life conditions, you are really re-evaluating your own value system, which influences the quality of your choices in life, including your sense of self-confidence and self-worth. In order to move forward in life, you must first recognize who you are and where you are in life, which is regulated in a large part by your value system.

You could feel challenged as well as excited during this time in your life. Your mind and beliefs could feel challenged by reviewing your life values, especially if you know it is going to create some foundational changes for. You could also feel excited because aliveness is based on change and renewal, and when you make changes, your enthusiasm for life is renewed. Both challenge and excitement are partners in change and bring great gifts of creativity and expansion, no matter how you feel.

Once you establish and recognize your true value system, it makes life so much easier because you can reference *your* value system in everything you do and decide how *you* want to spend your energy; choosing whatever brings you the greatest joy. This is true integrity, choosing and creating life from the inside out.

DIRECTIVES

This cycle is the perfect time to "unload" - get rid of the material possessions that no longer have meaning for you. If it is precious to you personally, keep it. If it is not, think of someone in your life that would love having you gift them with this item. Remember the saying, "one man's trash is another man's treasure". Lighten your material load and you lighten your mental, physical and emotional energy load. Everything you own, owns and uses your energy. If you claim ownership of anything, you become attached to that life form and your energy will be used to sustain and be a part of that connection.

Now more than ever in your life, recall and reclaim your energy for your health, aliveness, joy, exploration, and adventure and be willing to let go of possessions, relationships, and conditions in your life that use up your energy and bring nothing in return for your energy invested. This is not randomly discarding relationships or anything else in your life, it is simply becoming aware of everything in your life, in terms of aliveness. . . .the exchange of breath. If you honestly choose what works for your heart and soul, no matter how it looks or feels, everyone wins because inner truth is impartial.

Evaluate your life through the universal laws of movement, change and space. Everything is energy and information and the universal laws for energy on this planet are movement, change and space. All life is movement. Lack of *movement* is death or dying. Movement generates *change* for all forms of life. Without movement and change, your relationship with *space* becomes stagnant and no new life can enter.

If you do not make space in your lungs by releasing your breath, there is no space for the renewed breath to come in. Your life is renewed with every breath you receive and release. The breath in creates *movement* in your physical body, it is (ex)*changed* for the "old" breath and released to *space*. As long as you are in a body you are subject to the influence of these universal laws, known or unknown to you.

FOCUS

- **Self assessment**

  This is done from the inside out. What is it you really want out of life? It is never too late to set your intention, make your decisions and take steps of action to fulfill your desires.

- **Courage to change**

  Even though we are incredibly resilient beings, we are addicted to familiarity. To fulfill your heart's desires, you must be willing to change your life.

- **Acceptance of your choices**

There is only one person you have to live with every day of your life--YOU. Accept your desires and allow yourself the joy of meeting your personal needs and not feeling guilty.

QUESTIONS AND GUIDELINES

1. Is the energy in your life moving and are you feeling alive?

2. If not, why not?

3. If yes, what do you want to do to increase your aliveness?

4. From 1 - 10, what is your number that represents your willingness to try something new everyday in your life?

5. Can you look at yourself in the mirror, eye to eye, and say, "I deeply love and appreciate myself?"

6. If not, rub your forehead to release your resistance and reluctance, then vigorously tap your breastbone at the heart level for 10 times while you are saying out loud, "I deeply love and appreciate myself."

7. Now look in the mirror again as you did in #5. What happens now? Practice this until it brings you joy to look yourself in the eye and make this statement.

65 to 67½ Years

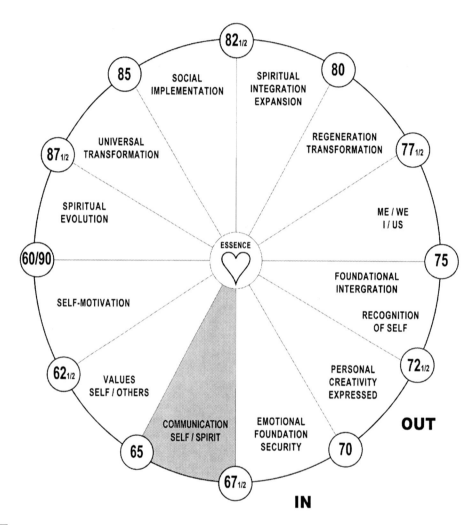

THEME

    Communication
       Personal
       Spiritual
    Self-trust

Chapter 30

Communication

POWER

There are only so many notes in an octave. Those notes get used over and over throughout the world to create new musical sounds every day. The reason that is possible is because different people use the same notes in a different way, with a different rhythm with different instruments. The same is true for words: we have to use them differently and then our communication can become creative and personalized to represent our true self as much as words are capable of doing that.

This cycle can be such a great adventure without even leaving your recliner or your house. All you have to do is listen to your self as you think or speak and then ask your self if what you just said is true for your heart as well. If not, listen to your heart's desires and let your heart have a voice and then you can speak the words that represent your truth when you are communicating with others. People sense when you are authentic and speaking "your truth." Be impeccable with your word. This is what I think Don Miguel Ruiz is referring to in his book, The Four Agreements.

Even if others do not like to hear your truth because of their own emotional response, they can still have more respect and trust for you because they can sense you have no hidden agenda. In other words, you are walking your talk. Living your truth.

Your truth is exciting and a great adventure that does not cost you thousands of dollars and is available to you everyday wherever you are. You can go beyond the imprisonment of your belief systems. Your conscious mind uses your trained belief systems as a map for your lifestyle and behavior, until you create an active intimate partnership with your heart. When this partnership takes place, your doorway to your soul is reopened at a whole new level of awareness and your relationship with all life takes on new and expanded meaning.

VULNERABILITY

Your sense and illusion of separation is strongly influenced as early as the 5 - 7½ year cycle when your conscious mind is enrolled in consistent academic training in order to learn the alphabet, read, write, work with numbers and all the necessary tools to be a linear thinker. It is very valuable to have strong linear skills in life and yet not at the sake of abandoning your heart and soul connection. That is like having a huge oak tree with no root system. It cannot live and sustain its life force for very long nor reach its greatest potential. Because this linear training is strong, consistent and comes at an early age, it is deeply imprinted in your neurological system and has a deep influence on your sense of self and your belief systems.

Whether these imprints are conscious or unconscious in your current experience, you can clear these patterns by using these very sophisticated tools to assist and guide you. You can clear your neuro-pathways of any imprints recorded at any age, at any time in your life. (www.universalhealthmethod.com or www.emofree.com)

DISCOVERIES

Have you ever listened to yourself talk to make sure you believe what you are saying? Your conscious mind is so porous and receptive to the input and influence you have received throughout your lifetime from everything and everyone you have come in contact with, consciously or unconsciously. If the input has been consistent enough, you "record" this information in your conscious or unconscious mind and "play it back" as if it were your own thoughts or truth.

Now is the time in your life when you really want to listen to what got recorded in your conscious and unconscious mind that has generated the belief system you use and influences the choices you make in your life. Are you getting the results your heart desires? If not, you may be using someone else's belief system to abort your own passion and joy in life. This is so common for all of us that I recognize it is a foundational and collective influence: we all have acquired some degree of belief conditioning unless we are born enlightened or attain enlightenment in this lifetime. This is another example of our interconnectedness through the consciousness and unconsciousness of the collective. You can approach this time of change with resentment or excitement. Your choice in recovering your own truth will dramatically influence your experience of change in your life.

Most languages create a limitation on creativity. Creativity is time less, form less and direction less. Language provides a structure that translates creativity into form through words. Without the structure of words we would not have books, songs, plays, movies, etc. Regardless of what language(s) you speak, the culture, traditions and values that are represented through the language will influence your thinking and beliefs. This is unavoidable and can be changed as you discover your personal values and choose to use different ways of communicating in the world. It is important to have integrity in the way you use your words to make sure they really represent you and your personal truth, otherwise you are like a parrot, repeating what has been repeated to you over and over in your life time.

Your heart is your "soul mate." It is the direct avenue of receptivity and communication with the Divine. You already have your soul mate, living inside of you, being ignored by your conscious mind most of the time because your heart's voice is soft and different than what you were taught to listen to through the spoken word. Everything is energy and information, and the spoken word is the most confined way you have of sharing this energy and information. When you actively participate in a relationship with your heart, you are in relationship with your soul: you get there by listening, not by thinking and talking.

DIRECTIVES

This cycle is the time to really question and assess your language, communication or lack of communication with your inner self and how you use words to manage your relating in life. Let's examine what this means for your everyday world.

When you were 5 - 7½ you were actively using the skills you started learning when you entered school. Your linear mind was very busy with all the daily activities that you were absorbing and involved in at that age. Your openness and vulnerability as a child did not do much filtering of information that you were receiving and experiencing. For many, this cycle marks the beginning of "overshadowing your heart and soul," which starts to veil your personal truth.

At 35 - 37½ you were definitely making different decisions and communicating at a different level. You have 30 years of experience and life situations influencing your choices. This could include a lot more "shadowing of consciousness" or a lot more unveiling which supported you to see your life differently than when you were 5 - 7½.

Now at 65 - 67½, you have the wonderful opportunity of bringing increased balance into your life by having more time and interest in listening to your heart and soul and to have the courage to follow your inner guidance and wisdom. This is the perfect time in your life to create balance between your conscious mind and your heart and soul.

FOCUS

- **Renew your curiosity**

Question your life, reality and beliefs with innocence and curiosity. These are the qualities of consciousness that keep you connected to your inner wisdom. If you don't think you have to "know everything" you can be open to new beginnings.

- **Trust your inner wisdom**

  Your inner voice is a valid source of wisdom. You have lived with this voice your whole Life; receive this support in joy and acceptance of your deep inner power and wisdom.

- **Tell the truth**

  Give yourself permission to acknowledge and accept how you really feel and then make choices in your life to live and support these beliefs and desires. Walk your talk.

QUESTIONS AND GUIDELINES

1. When you were 5 - 7½, what inner playmates or dreams did you give up?

2. What have you believed for years in your heart and your head said, "No way, Impossible?"

3. Do you believe in a higher power? a god? a divine being? a divine force?

4. What is your trust level that you are personally important in this divine force?

5. What do you consider your benefits in life to have your heart and mind work together as soul mates?

6. Do you trust what you believe? If not, what needs to change so you can?

7. Do you trust what your heart knows? If not, why not?

8. Do you trust your intuition? If not, what is your fear in trusting your intuition?

67½ to 70 Years

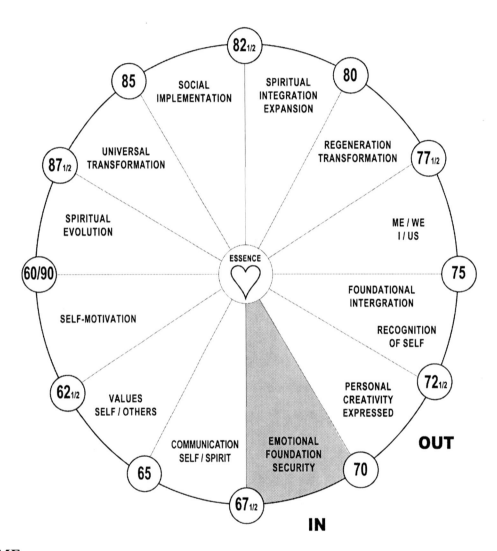

THEME

Emotional transformation
Emotional stability
Emotional needs

Chapter 31

Emotional Foundation

POWER

Emotion is energy in motion. The universal principle of all life on this planet is movement, change and space. As a human being, you are contracted to the same universal principles, as is all life on planet earth. Recognizing and claiming your inner power through your emotional body empowers you to be an active co-creator with the universe. It is imperative that you are a conscious co-creator, for life and living, or you may be an unconscious creator of death and dying.

When a flower begins to blossom, its destiny is to blossom fully. You are the flower in your life and it is time to fully blossom. In order to open your heart and embrace all the richness of life, it is important to accept all parts of your life as divine. No matter how you feel now or have felt about your choices and experiences throughout your life, you can bring everything home to your heart, through love, and let it be transformed. Love is the essence of life that sustains and supports you mentally, physically, emotionally and spiritually.

Love is a force field of power, not just a sentiment, and within that force field, all life is renewed. This renewal is what you often hear referred to as "unconditional love". The renewal of all life is unconditional through love.

VULNERABILITY

As human beings, we live in a body with a conscious and unconscious mind empowered emotionally and enfolded in the power of Spirit, the Divine. An amazing thing happens in "civilized cultures." We get very disassociated from our emotions and somehow manage to believe "emotions are our enemy" or at best "unsafe" for us to experience, so our mission is to control those emotions, keep them hidden. This split in our thinking creates a lifetime of discomfort feeling separated from a divine part of us. Either every aspect of our humanness evolves from a divine source or it does not. We do not go shopping at Sears and Roebuck for our human self. We are a universal package, a divine and unique expression of life. The whole package is divine, including our emotions.

In America we have been trained to measure the value of things in life by the way they feel. We are especially enrolled in whatever will make us happy. We will buy it, try it, wear it, eat it, drive it, do it. . . . . you name it, we are in line.

Since there is a huge range of emotions that do not feel good and do not make us feel happy, theses emotions get relegated to the "denial pile" - get rid of these, go away from these, don't claim or feel these. So we spend a huge part of our life trying to get away from "these feelings" or trying to "understand" them or find out where they come from? A common question is, "What am I supposed to do with these feelings?" If we don't know what to do with these feelings, it seems logical to deny that they even exist.

Emotions are an experience, registered in your body; they are not an intellectual process. Emotions are energy in motion. Your conscious mind can become a director of this energy and be a support in managing your emotional power that influences the choices you make and thus your behavior. If you attempt to ignore your emotions through your thinking, these emotions become heavy burdens on your heart and will dramatically influence your quality of life. Suppressed emotions diminish your life force, never enhancing nor increasing your aliveness. Suppressed emotions are a precursor to disease.

Now is the time to recognize if you are denying your emotions and decide the quality of life you desire to create; determine how denied emotions influence your behavior in creating the life that you want.

DISCOVERIES

I am sure you have heard these phrases before: "It's never too late to have a happy childhood," "Life begins at 30, 40 50, etc". All of these are just words until "something drops in" and you *feel* your foundation based on what you have heard or believed. Everything is possible, and it is created according to your belief system. You are the director and projector of your life movie. The Universe delivers through the structure you create in your mind, according to your thinking and beliefs. Be prepared during this cycle to drop deeper into your heart and be "in the feelings of life," no longer able to stand on the edge of emotions trying to understand what is happening through your mind. Thinking your feelings and feeling your feelings are two different experiences.

During the 7½ - 10 cycle, if your emotional foundation was not developed in a healthy family situation, your emotions may have been fragmented, wounded, denied, traumatized or buried from your consciousness. (See Chapter 7.)

Your emotions can remain in these conditions until some aspect of life comes to the door of these stagnated, imprisoned parts and says, "time to wake up, everybody move out". Many times wake up calls come through a crisis. Crisis is the ultimate call in life when everything in our world crashes and we are forced to think and behave differently; to wake up completely and feel life fully, even for a moment, an hour, a few days or weeks.

Passing through this cycle again at 37½ - 40 presented another opportunity to review your emotional foundation and reclaim and recover more of the suppressed or hidden emotions from your childhood. You can celebrate your 30 years of living and what life has provided for you to learn and grow emotionally.

Now here you are again, at 67½ - 70, the third time around in the same cycle providing yet another perception of your emotional foundation. You have more experiences and more time now to understand and accept yourself and what you feel. This supports you to review and relish the nurturing emotions you have generated in your life.

Many of these changes are born from pain and discomfort, influencing your interactions with others you have met and loved along the way. All of this has added to your treasure chest of emotional empowerment.

You also have time to be with the emotions that have hung on through the years, causing you a sense of sadness, aloneness, hopelessness, frustrations, etc. Forgiveness or acceptance may be a key to releasing these feelings to a new level of expression in your life. This includes forgiving yourself first and then forgiving others; which is a natural result and response from self-forgiveness.

DIRECTIVES

This is the cycle to examine your home, family, and emotional foundation and emotional security. Look for any stuck, empty or fearful places so that you can reclaim and release any stagnant emotions and then use that released emotional power to make different choices to change your life experiences. Emotions are expressed and experienced in the 'present' moment, not your past or future - right here, right now, where your feet are. Emotions are energy in motion, and **never** regulated by time or age. Your emotions can be redirected and flow "where your focus goes" to direct this power; at any given moment that you decide to feel differently about something and take steps of action your life experience will change. You can have a different experience in life right now by making different choices of how you are going to relate to your emotions, no matter how long you have been feeling angry, stuck or any other feeling these neuro-pathways can be cleared. (See www.universalhealthmethod.com or www.emofree.com)

You owe this to yourself. Free yourself emotionally and you enrich the quality of your life. Every cell in your body can release stress, receive more oxygen and be filled with more life force. Emotionally you can with a greater sense of aliveness. As long as you have the gift of life, live it fully and be committed to release all the old ways that limit and confine your health, wellness, and joy in life.

During this cycle, the main movie you are in is the Feeling Movie. Do not let your mind be a mental dictator, acting as if your emotions are not important and that you do not "feel your emotions". Your emotional message or messenger will just get louder, until you create a crisis to get your attention. This is really a huge waste of your energy when choice is an option for another way of living.

Awaken each day, and before you get out of bed, bless your body, feel your breath moving through your body, greet the day in gratitude, **you are alive**. Celebrate life and aliveness all day and be conscious of feeling how wonderful it is to live and move and be alive, no matter what the day brings forth. You are the star and this is a good movie you are creating with each choice you make. You are the one that makes a difference in your life.

FOCUS

- **Forgive yourself and others**

  No matter what choices you made at any age, they were the best you knew how to make at that time. Forgive yourself and others and accept the blessing of the experience and the growth in your life.

- **Accept life as a gift**

  You are the gift in life. When you accept "you" as a gift, then all life can reveal itself as a gift, in unending ways. How you perceive and receive yourself is how you will perceive and receive the world.

- **Trust your ability to love**

  Love is a force field of power, not just a sentiment. Your life is an expression of love. Love is the unified filed for all life.

QUESTIONS AND GUIDELINES

1. What emotion/emotions are you most resistant to?

2. What will happen to you if you fully feel this/these emotions?

3. What will happen to you if you do not feel this/these emotions?

4. List 3-5 experiences in your life that are peak experiences and what feelings they generate for you.

5. Were these experiences in your life critical turning points for you?

6. Write a letter of forgiveness and acceptance of yourself.

7. Write a letter of forgiveness to someone in your life who you want to forgive. (Listen to your heart and determine if you need to mail it or burn it.) Even if this person is deceased, write the letter anyway and burn it the same day written.

8. Write a letter of love and appreciation to someone and let them know how you feel about them. (Listen to your heart and determine if you need to mail it or burn it.) Even if this person is deceased, write the letter anyway and burn it the same day written.

70 to 72½ Years

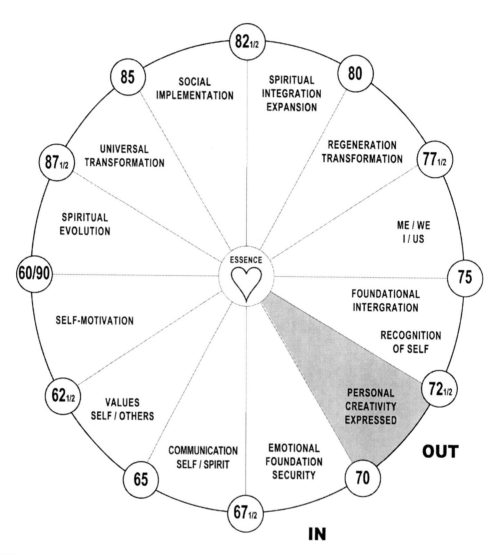

THEME

Expression
Creativity
Aliveness

226

Chapter 32

Personal Creativity

POWER

This cycle is about creative expressions in life: what makes you feel vitally alive, entertains you, and invites you to new possibilities in life? Sharing your creativity and wisdom with others, especially the children, renews your interest in life and expands your own potential. What is it that you really love doing and makes you feel vibrantly alive when you share it with others? This is the area you want to focus on in your life right now, sharing your joy. Joy is the vibrational door to your heart and soul. Many people feel alone and hopeless, living without any sense of joy, companionship or personal recognition.

You never know when your smile, or kind word may be the turning point for one in such despair. When you share your creativity and joy with the world, this allows your own energy to expand and renews your life, a win/win for everyone.

Our heart seeks happiness because we know joy is the doorway to our soul. Children live joyously in their life because they express from their heart and soul spontaneously until they become conditioned by life's experiences, which many times teaches them to hide their joy behind fear and sadness.

Be strong and courageous and try something new in your life--even if it feels frightening to you. Do it any way--just go for it! Remember as you try new things in your life you are giving expression to your divine inner child; you can always change your mind and choose something else if you discover that this choice really does not bring you joy or support you.

VULNERABILITY

The joy that is generated in childhood comes from your natural spontaneity and curiosity. Being born into this world of multiple possibilities generates a curiosity to explore and discover life, on every level, as a great adventure. If these qualities become suppressed in your life and you are reluctant to express your natural delight in life, then you begin to live in the shadow of fear, doubt and disappointment. No matter how long you have lived on this planet, it is still a world of wonder and there are always amazing things to discover and learn. If your experience in life is predetermined by the past, then you may have lost your sense of curiosity that ignites the possibility of discovery. This is not a good sign.

Isn't it amazing that at this age it takes courage to be curious and seek new adventures, when curiosity is a magnet to our future potential and our creativity?

DISCOVERIES

When you were 10 - 12½ years old (See Chapter 8), what did you really want to do at that age that you never got a chance to? Play drums, write a book, dance, travel, visit a relative, etc.

What about when you were 40 - 42½ years old? (See Chapter 20) What were your hearts desires that are still unfulfilled? Now is the time to focus on your "desires and creativity" and fill it up.

Do not let age be an excuse for your not being able to fulfill your desires.

Joy is the gateway to your soul; it is an abiding energy that never leaves your life even in time of great trauma or despair. Joy is like the sun--it is always there, even when you cannot see it or feel it. It is the magnet that invites life to renew itself, through birth, through breath, through beauty, through love and aliveness. Joy is a quantum-leap experience; a smile can give hope to a life, a shared hello can make someone's heart sing, and eye contact lets someone know they are not invisible in the world. *We are an interdependent species and we flourish when we interact with each other.*

Unless you choose to stifle your spontaneity and curiosity, every day of your life can be wondrous and a renewal through the joy and anticipation of the unknown, regardless of your age or your past history. By being open to receiving in your life right now, your aliveness, appreciation, gratitude and acceptance of today can continue to be an ever-increasing and enriching experience of unlimited possibilities for you.

DIRECTIVES

If for any reason your physical health presents a challenge to your spontaneity, then allow your curiosity to create avenues of discovery that suit your health needs. If you are alive and breathing and your mind is reading these words, you can be as alive as you are willing to be, no matter what. Search in the library, on the web, on video, with music-- whatever means you can access that will allow you to involve your life in discovery and relating with what others are doing in the world today, and how you might get involved.

Never underestimate the value of the smallest human contact with another, you never know where that person is emotionally or mentally, and you may be their ray of hope by your joy and presence in the grocery store line. Do not underestimate the value of your joyful, healthy life being a model of inspiration for someone. By the same token, if you are downhearted or feeling ill, allow someone to bless you with his or her joy and loving support. Life is a two way street. We all benefit when we share life with each other.

If joy were the vision and goal in life, individually and collectively, do you see how differently we would be living on this planet? You can create this reality in your own life regardless of what the world is doing. As human beings we always function best if we have a goal/destination. If living and sharing your joy becomes your motivation in life, then your daily choices may be very different than they were in the past, thus the outcome will also be different. This is how you change the future: **today** you make different choices. It doesn't take a rocket scientist to discern if what you are thinking, choosing, or doing creates a sense of joy or the possibility of joy in your life. And if it does not, why are you investing your energy in it? What is the reward? Joy is a huge reward that is not dependent on what the rest of the world is or is not doing.

Most of the time you have the most fun when you are sharing your adventure in life with others. Participate in activities that fulfill your desire to create and experience your joy by doing it with others who have a similar interest. Enjoy sharing together and do not compare your creativity with any other person. Your creativity is unique because you created it, and creativity is not on the profit and loss sheet of life. It doesn't have to make sense or please anyone else, it just has to bring you joy. All creativity is priceless, an expression of the divine.

Creativity is born in stillness and receptivity. Go for walks by yourself or with others in silence, meditate, listen to music you love, be with nature and listen to Her voice speak to your heart. In the stillness, new life is born.

Commit to yourself that every day of your life you will create and experience at least one thing that brings you joy. Have this as your goal, and this alone will take you on the greatest adventure – being alive and loving your life.

Spirit has placed a dream in your heart for a better world,
starting with your family, extending to your work, community,
country and stretching beyond your nation.
Speak your truth and inspire others, for your are meant to make
a significant and sizable difference.

Mary Manin Morrissey

FOCUS

• **Expression**

Find something you have never done, and try it out. Your inner creativity is unlimited and will express in amazing ways if given the opportunity.

• **Pleasure**

What are some simple, ordinary things that you can experience in your daily life that really bring pleasure to you, and chances are, will extend and bring pleasure to others.

• **Aliveness**

Aliveness is the key to your wellness, mentally, physically, emotionally and spiritually. Give yourself permission to feel your aliveness and allow that power to generate your choices in life.

QUESTIONS AND GUIDELINES

1. Do you recognize and appreciate your talents, your gifts?

2. List 5 creative talents/gifts you recognize about yourself.

3. Now make a corresponding list of where and with whom you can share each of these talents and gifts.

4. Create a schedule for yourself to determine the time frame in which you will support yourself to express and share these talents and gifts with those you have chosen.

5. Have you thought about being a mentor and sharing your wisdom of life with those needing your loving support?

6. What creative experience is missing in your life?

7. Go on an adventure and discover how you can fulfill this desire for yourself.

72½ to 75 Years

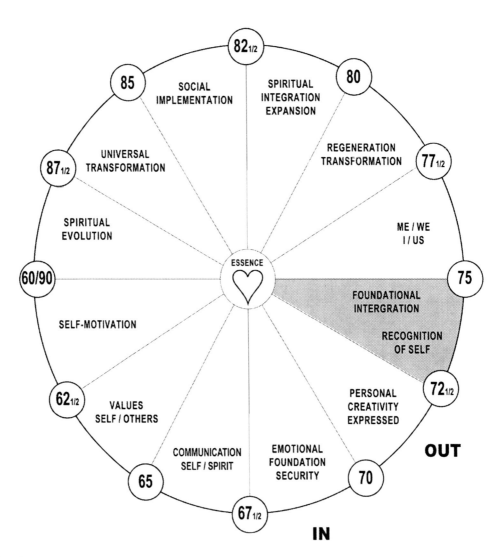

THEME

Integration
Stabilizing
Strengthening

Chapter 33

Integration

POWER

This is the cycle of the master weaver. During this cycle all the changes that have occurred in your life since you were 60-years old are now ready to be consciously woven into a new foundation in preparation for the years from 75 - 90. This is a layered weaving because you are integrating all the lifestyles that you have been living since you were 12½ years old (See Chapter 9), the first time you were in this cycle. The second time was from 42½ - 45 (See Chapter 21). If you review those cycles in your life and the changes you made, it gives you an idea of the lifestyle that you developed out of these significant cycles in your life.

You are experiencing life on more levels than your conscious mind understands and many times even believes in. Everything is energy and information and so are you, and you are relating to everything else in the universe that is energy and information. The unspoken language of energy is your guiding light for all life.

From birth to 15, you develop your personal mental, emotional, spiritual and physical foundation that you will be using for the rest of your life. From 30 to 45 you come through this passage of life cycles again and review and revise, consciously or unconsciously, your lifestyle and the foundation you are using. This is the third time through, from 60 to 75, with three layers of life to weave together at this time, different than ever before, because you are new in this moment of your life experience. You have never been here before at this age. It is a very precious time because age allows another level of perception that does not come in your youth.

Once you begin to review your life, there is an unraveling that begins to reveal many treasures, empty places, possibilities, hidden dreams and much more that you may never have touched on before. Receive this time in your life with excitement. It is a time of celebration for who you are and for your intended future.

VULNERABILITY

As you review your life, and particularly the last 15 years, do so with appreciation and wonderment, not judgment. Every decision you have made your whole life was the best and clearest choice you knew how to make at that time. Today you know more about yourself and life than ever before. It is unfair and unkind to take today's wisdom and evaluate yesterday's choices.

If you measure yesterday's choices as a mile marker to compare how you have progressed in your life today, you never need to feel like a loser. When you can appreciate the movement and change you have created during your lifetime that you may not have acknowledged at the time of your experience, you can begin to fill in some of the "blanks" in your life with acceptance, recognition, appreciation, and forgiveness. Consciously reviewing your life allows you to experience your life as a rite of passage – release the past and celebrate the present.

DISCOVERIES

This cycle is a rite of passage from a foundational process to a presentation process: recognizing yourself and who you are now guides how you will be sharing your unique life experience with others in your social circle.

Living in a culture that is not tribal in nature nor participating with rites of passage at special times in life, your life and the circumstances you experience daily become your rites of passage. A rite of passage is a conscious use of the energy to change or focus power and transformation in a desired direction that is life enhancing and supportive. When you are living your life without the awareness that your daily life process is your rite of passage you do not get to have the conscious benefit of this change. This influences your perception of your own personal power and often influences your sense of self-esteem, self-confidence and accomplishment.

The basic foundational magnetism from 60-years on is the call from your heart and soul to spiritually "come home." Come home to your personal truth, your soul commitments and have the clarity and courage to live these truths: to be willing to take your place as an elder/mentor for those who are seeking your wisdom. To share what you have learned by living is the ultimate rite of passage.

Your greatest commitment to aliveness is to stay open, willing to change and remain excited about each day as a precious gift and celebrate each day by being willing to love and be loved.

Gratitude and appreciation are life-enriching qualities and the more you can experience your life with these attitudes, the richer your life will be mentally, physically, emotionally and spiritually.

DIRECTIVES

As you are weaving your foundation from the richness of your life experiences, one question you can ask yourself to help you determine how you want to direct your life for the next 15 years is "What am I spending my life energy on? Is this supporting me to achieve what I truly want in my life?" Every day you invest your life and energy in some way, and most of that expenditure is unconscious which can create disappointment if you are not creating what you truly desire for your personal fulfillment. Power flows where your focus goes. Your conscious intention is the greatest assurance in life that you can change the way that you experience your world, regardless of what others say or do.

FOCUS

- **Expand Awareness**

   No matter how you have thought or felt about something in your life, expand your awareness and look at it differently. Enroll your curiosity to explore possibilities for change.

- **Make new choices**

   Life is about choice and change. Consciously make a choice, use it for a day and see what happens in your life. This may be the first step to a new way of thinking and living.

- **Experience life as wonderment**

   Begin to look at the world and life as a hologram. We all breathe the same breath. Let the mystery of life unveil itself for you by being open daily to new life options.

QUESTIONS AND GUIDELINES

1. Do you have "hidden desires" for your life that you refuse to accept because they seem impossible?

2. What will happen if you explore the possibility of participating with these desires?

3. What fears come up?

4. What doubts come up?

5. What beliefs come up and undermine your self-confidence to explore fulfilling these desires?

6. What do you believe and hold onto about yourself that is limiting and confining your creative expression in life?

7. Would you be interested in letting go of these limitations and experience what happens to the quality of your life?

75 to 77½ Years

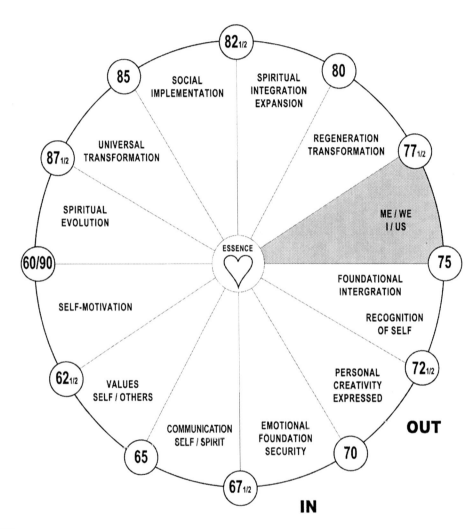

THEME

Relating
One on one
      Business
      Friendship
      Personal Partnerships

Chapter 34

Personal Relating

POWER

Everything in life is relating to everything else. This is a universal law of life, and yet we humans act as if it is a negotiable item. Relating is not a negotiable item in life. It is a way of life. What is negotiable is the *quality of relating* that we do with humans, the environment, ecology, all life known and unknown to us. Sometimes our deepest pain and our greatest joy stem from the same place -- personal relationships.

When you review your life cycles as a continuum of learning experiences in the University of Life, you can very easily detect the blessings you may have missed as you lived your life until now. Part of the blessing of consciously using the *Wheel Of Life Cycles* is it presents consistent guidelines in your life and gives you permission to really recognize what specific classroom of life you are in right now and determine how you want to participate, knowing "this too shall pass" because in 2½ years you enter another cycle.

This is the cycle to examine the quality of your relating experiences and consciously increase that quality for yourself and with others. The richness of life increases dramatically as the quality of your relating experiences take on greater depth and meaning for you.

VULNERABILITY

Part of what makes relating stay alive is the willingness to change and grow in your personal life and with each person you are relating with. Life on this planet is about everything changing, so there is nothing that can remain the same. In relationships that provide you comfort or nurturing, you might be fearful of change, especially if the change feels like any sense of loss or separation. Living in appreciation of yourself and recognizing who you are supports your gratitude and appreciation for yourself and others.

If you are in relationships that feel conflicted or unloving, you could feel fearful that this will never change. Nothing changes without taking steps of action. Make sure your choices for action are heart based decisions. When you change the way you relate to your thoughts, words and actions with yourself and others, you will experience your life feeling different even if the circumstances seem the same. Life changes from the inside out, even if it is catalyzed by outside experiences. It changes according to the choices you make in relationship to the circumstance or person.

DISCOVERIES

If you will give yourself permission to participate in all relationships as a classroom you can release yourself from huge levels of emotional distress. When you recognize the main class in your life is personal self-discovery, then you can give up the need to understand the other person or the apparent conditions and focus on what is your lesson, what are you feeling. You can **never** understand what another is thinking or feeling; you are challenged enough just trying to recognize and understand what you feel. If you take a step back and can look at the situation at hand from a more objective or impersonal view, emerging insights and awareness can then increase your options for successful or workable relating experiences in your life and reduce your emotional stress and control issues.

Relating is a life-long classroom and you will continue to learn more about yourself and others in every relationship. If you recognize relating as a classroom, then you understand that as long as you are alive, you are going to be participating in this classroom and constantly learning something new everyday of your life. If the same disruptive patterns or behaviors keep coming up in your relationships, it is easy to get disenchanted and feel it is too much work to be able to relate successfully and joyously. When the goal is to increase the quality of your relating experiences for yourself and others, each situation is another opportunity to grow and learn together, even if it feels challenging.

A pivotal point in relating is getting attention and giving attention. You must have attention to survive; it is a primal need for human beings. The way in which you were motivated to get attention from birth to 2½ years old (See Chapter 4, 16 & 28) is your foundational imprint for getting attention throughout your life unless you modify this behavior, consciously or unconsciously, through the choices you make in your relating experiences.

At 15 -17½ (See Chapter 10) you practice getting your needs met in relationships and discovering what you need to do to have relating be fun so you can feel safe enough to express and experience yourself with another. At this age you may have made decisions that revised your attention-getting behaviors from infancy.

Forty-five to 47½ (See Chapter 22) was another review of relationships and what you really wanted and what the relationships in your life were requiring of you in order to feel that they were valuable and mutually beneficial. Here you are again at 75 to 77 ½, with another wonderful opportunity to assess your relationship desires and how you can get these fulfilled and have quality relating experiences.

DIRECTIVES

You have to consciously choose to improve the quality of your relationships or they will "take the path of least resistance" which is the habit pattern for relating that you have learned and used your whole life, whether it is satisfying or not.

In order to make choices for change, it is helpful to have some idea of what you want. This is where you need to be clear on the qualities in relating that are important to you.

What makes you feel good and motivates you to more aliveness?

Let yourself clearly assess the person/persons you are relating to and see if you share these qualities. If not, you can begin to explore what you need to do to increase the quality of your relationships and be willing to do that. This may include being willing to stop relating to some people in your life in the same way or make changes that will allow new ways of relating for all concerned.

FOCUS

- **Quality in relating**

  What is really important to you in your relationships now? Decide what a quality relationship feels like to you and create your relationships to match that desire.

- **Forgiveness**

  When those memories flash through and you wish you would have done or said something differently, forgive yourself and then allow that forgiveness to be extended everyone involved.

- **Acceptance**

  Release your agenda on yourself and others on how you "should be." Learn to love and accept who you really are, which allows you to have acceptance of others and who they really are. You cannot give to another what you do not give to yourself.

QUESTIONS AND GUIDELINES

1. Inventory your current relationships. Make a plus column and a minus column. For each person review your relationship and place the qualities you recognize in the plus or minus column. What do you recognize?

2. What adjustments do you need to make in each relationship to increase the quality of this relationship for you?

3. Are you willing to allow some of your relationships to shift position in your life if they are not the quality you desire?

4. Have your needs in relationships changed? How?

5. Do you understand where your responsibility ends and the other person's begins when making changes in relationship? (See *Co-Dependent No More* by Melodie Beattie.)

6. Is there anyone, including yourself, that you need to release through forgiveness?

7. Are you willing to allow that release to be returned to compassion and love now?

77½ to 80 Years

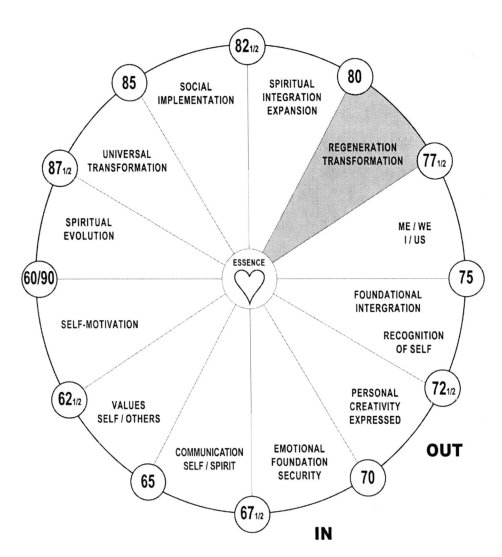

THEME

    Self- empowerment
    Emerging power
    Personal and collective power

Chapter 35

Spiritual Transformation

POWER

Life is a circle. When you are born you arrive in the natural circle of life, conception, gestation, birth. You breathe in, you breathe out. You are born into a body; you die and release the body. You eat and assimilate food and you eliminate the remains. The never-ending circle of life is the foundation for all life.

The circle of life is the power of life. It is based on an interconnected force field that is unified and supports all forms of life. Einstein spent the last 30 years of his life studying the principle of the unified field. This cycle is calling you to return to the power of life, relating to life as an on-going, experience rather than just a thought process. This is a state of being similar to the simplicity and pureness of your infancy.

Notice how our bodies change as we "get older." Our eyes start changing and do not want to "look at the small stuff," so we get reading glasses. Then our ears decide to filter out a lot of that "noise of life," so we get hearing aids. Our mind decides there are a lot of meaningless pieces of information that are unnecessary so we "forget"--we no longer store information in our memory bank in the same way. Can you see there is a natural way of living that releases you from many of the developed conditions of your life that may have interfered with your recognizing and being in the circle of life consciously? This is not a dis-empowering time of your life, it is a very empowering time of your life. A lot of the habits and conditions that you developed during your life and accepted as your reality are overshadowing your naturalness.

VULNERABILITY

The more linear you become as you are growing up, the farther removed your mind can become from your heart and soul, unless you are consciously clearing the debris of socialization. When the conscious mind (1/8) becomes the dictator of your reality, it subjects your (7/8) heart and soul power to a subservient position. . . .sometimes having no voice at all in your daily reality. This lack of relationship with your heart and soul can create a life of tension and struggle: you are not living in harmony within your own life or within the circle of life.

Because a life of tension and stress accumulates on a daily basis, you may not be consciously aware of how much stress and tension you live with each day. Your body has built-in regulators that register your stress and tension levels. When these levels accumulate and reach extreme conditions that affect your physical health, your body responds with physical symptoms: headaches, migraines, backaches, illness, disease, digestive challenges, dizziness, tiredness, becoming accident prone, depression, etc.

Not only will this tension and stress put your physical condition into a state of reaction, the same thing happens with your mind and your emotions. Sooner or later, every part of you rebels when under stress. This may be a life saving "wake up call" to help you become conscious of the conditions in your body, mind and emotions, that you may be unaware of, so you can begin to make healthy choices. Every part of your body, mind and emotions is designed to express aliveness on every level, even if you have been influenced by life conditions that promote the illusion of separation and which promotes disease and dying. Life is full of challenging events for human beings so it is pretty safe to say, all humans are stressed at some level after birth.

Living in a state of tension and stress creates inner conflict that usually manifests itself in your personal relationships and your extended relationships: partner, children, family, business, community and nation. As you manage your inner conflicts and your tension and stress you will relate and behave differently in the world. This is the only direct contribution you can make to influence peace in the world. Find peace in your own life, in your own heart and mind and then you become a living demonstration of peace by just living your life. All life benefits when you feel peaceful.

DISCOVERIES

You do not have to understand everything in life in order to have meaning in your life. As far as we know, humans are the only species using a linear mind allowing us to learn languages, spelling, math, directions, construct buildings and highways, cook a meal, brush our teeth, drink water and unlimited other actions. Your inner and innate intelligence that you were born with is an eternal connection to all life. You always have access to that inner wisdom no matter your age or how much you have been conditioned during your life to just listen to your mind.

In your infancy, you are immersed in your inner wisdom; your head and heart are not conflicted. In your developing and adult years you may feel conflicted, inside and out, when your linear mind is trained to override and ignore your inner wisdom. At any time in your life you can begin to recapture the magic of living united with your head and heart. The pure state of being that you are as an infant is eternally awaiting your recognition, acceptance and participation, no matter what your age.

In this cycle, the call to return to the circle of life consciously is stronger than it ever was when you were here before at 17½ - 20 (Chapter 11) or 47½ - 50 years old. (Chapter 23) If you are discovering that many of your beliefs, thoughts, attitudes, behaviors and conditions in life that felt so important during these previous cycles and ages are not feeling as important any more, recognize and accept this as progress in your consciousness. As a matter of fact this is called recovery. This can be a relief to finally give yourself permission to let go of the illusions of separation and conflict that you have learned and return to your naturalness. Remember, recovery as it is in process may not feel like a "good thing" or the strength you are seeking. Go through the recovery process, pass through the hallway of change, and allow yourself to come out on the other end. . . . .a different person. You will be really happy with your commitment to see this "thing" through. You will have a strong sense of accomplishment and added confidence in yourself.

DIRECTIVES

Your challenge over the years is to change your value system from the outer values of life to the inner values of life. This is another blessing of aging, you can more easily recognize what really matters to you at this time in your life. You have lived long enough to know what is most important to you. Allow yourself to listen to your heart and soul and create your life experiences from your inner awareness and inner values.

This is a very special and empowering cycle in your life when you let go of society's expectations of you and listen to your inner wisdom first and live according to those guidelines. You will notice an enriched and increasingly relaxed state of life happening for you when you give yourself permission to once again have an intimate relationship with your inner wisdom. Trust YOU! The love that you are has guided you throughout your life and continues to do so now. Relaxing is not dying, and it does not mean that you are lazy or irresponsible; it is actually life enhancing and allows more and more of your wellness and joy to emerge on a daily basis. This is a good investment of your life force for the fulfillment of your dreams and visions. Taking good care of you is the best investment in your life.

FOCUS

- **Inner Strength**

  Trust your inner awareness, intuition, inner guidance...that is your innate natural power you were born with and it has guided you throughout your life, whether you were conscious of this power of not.

- **Let Go**

Life is flow, circulation, movement. Allow yourself to have more of this experience in your life, mentally, physically, emotionally and spiritually.

- **Renew commitments**

Live in gratitude and acceptance of each life experience. Everything in life brings rewards and blessings if you open your heart and mind and allow divine timing to reveal that truth to you, allow the time to "receive the blessings".

QUESTIONS AND GUIDELINES

1. What does "circle of life" mean to you?
2. Are you fully claiming your inner power and aliveness?
3. If not, why not?
4. List 3 dreams or visions you have always desired to experience in your life.
5. Commit to one of them and begin to live it now.
6. List 3 conditions in life that you want to be released from.
7. Name five qualities of yours that you recognize as valuable.
8. How can you increase these qualities in your life and expand your sense of aliveness, pleasure and fulfillment?

80 to 82½ Years

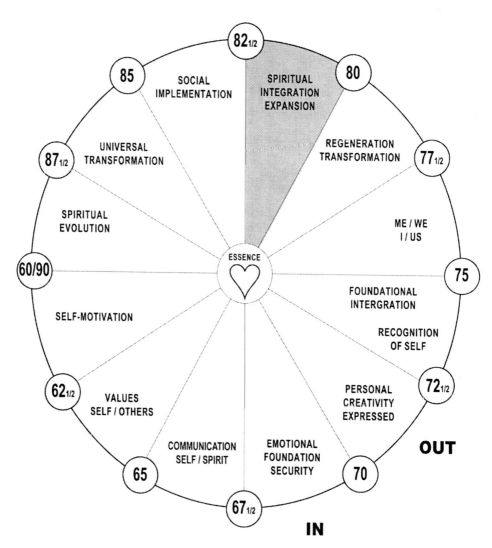

THEME

Inspiration
International awareness
Natural rhythm

Chapter 36

Inspiration

POWER

All life seeks the Light. You are a living expression of the Light. Every cell floats in a sea of energy and the field of energy around each cell increases with meditation, prayer, positive intentions and actions. What you think and believe truly influences the quality of your life from the inside out. In this cycle, the Light that you are is seeking greater and greater expression: freedom from socially imposed belief systems that do not match your inner truth.

In the Divine Plan of life, everything works for your highest good, and the measurement of the value of your experience is not based on your emotional response to it. You can review and recognize in your life that many of your most powerful and life-changing experiences were also your most challenging or painful. Every choice you made in your life was made from the highest place you knew at the time the choice was needed. Be generous in your compassion with yourself when you review your life experiences. You did the best that you knew how to do at that time in your life. Measuring yesterday's choices with today's awareness is not a fair comparison and it will surely mean, you will loose in yesterday's decisions and experiences, when in fact they are part of the fertilizer necessary for you to continue to blossom your entire life.

VULNERABILITY

Any time you choose to step outside the "box of tradition, the familiar," you will feel your fears and probably be challenged by the fears of others. Even though change is the key ingredient in all life, your fears challenge and resist change because there is a part of you that knows you will be living in an unfamiliar way. Familiar is comfortable, even if it is not necessarily healthy or balanced. Comfort feels safe, even if it could be stagnating for your life. Without the events of life, you would probably stay with comfort rather than increase your sense of discomfort through fear to go into some lifestyle that is unfamiliar. Unfamiliar is aliveness. There is more happening in this universe that is unfamiliar to our human mind than is familiar. To openly live with and embrace this reality you increase your sense of aliveness and harmony with all life, even if it does feel scary.

You "crack the egg of consciousness" by openly and consistently questioning your lifestyle, belief systems, values, behaviors, attitudes, actions, choices, relationships, religious beliefs, the laws of nature, man-made laws, organizations and institutions. In this process of discovery you begin to allow your soul blueprint to have a more direct influence in your life by increasing your heart and mind connection with your deep inner wisdom. Even though this puts you into unfamiliar territory in your thinking and believing, it opens up the door for pure potential to emerge through you as your heart and soul express and inspire others by sharing your dreams and visions. We are all in this movie of life together. No one has your starring role and cannot possibly know your dreams and visions if you do not recognize them or share them with us.

DISCOVERIES

The circle of life moves as a spiral and throughout your life cycles you will participate in many areas of your life from a different perspective. When you visited this cycle for the first time, you were 20 - 22½ years old. (Chapter 12) Remember what that time was like for you? What were you impassioned about? What kind of relationship did you have with God? Buddha? Religion? Philosophy? Universal consciousness? How did all of that change by the time you came through this cycle again at 50 - 52½? (Chapter 24) Now here you are again in this same cycle, and life is encouraging you to become even more deeply introspective and inquisitive about your beliefs and your ideas that are beyond general conversation and awareness: What is life all about? What is the biggest difference you notice about yourself as you enter this cycle this time compared to how you looked at life and your philosophy and values in the previous cycles?

This cycle recalls and reclaims the awareness that your future is determined by the choices you make today. By making today's choices more congruent and harmonious with your heart and soul, and using the rich wisdom gleaned from your past, you can create a future that could feel more authentic and fulfilling. This cycle is a call to your heart and soul to release your inner and emerging visions. Dare to listen to your heart and soul and the possibilities that you hear and see. This is how all change takes place in life: first you have awareness, then a desire driven by a passion to create change and then steps of action to make that desire a reality.   Take a risk!!! There is no future without vision and imagination, hopes and dreams, and the courage to follow your heart.

The magic of dreams and visions is never confined by age, gender, religious affiliation, culture, intellect, beauty, position, power, money or anything else except your own mental limitations, judgments and conditions you learned to place on yourself. It takes courage to be in an intimate relationship with your dreams and visions and share them with other like-minded friends and be willing to change as the dreams and visions continue to grow. Having a strong support group that you trust to encourage you, as you need it, is a great comfort while you are transforming your belief systems.

DIRECTIVES

Questioning life, in every area, is a natural motivator and inspiration in this cycle: go beyond the man-made laws, examine the universal laws and imagine life without man-made limitations. Inspiration calls life to higher levels of potential.

Whatever you can do, or dream you can,
Begin it.
Boldness has genius, power, and magic in it.
Begin it now!

Johan Wolfgang von Goethe

History allows us to trace our choices and assess the value or error of those choices. When you look at your past, look with loving eyes and as an observer so you can assess the choices and direction created by your choices and derive the maximum benefit from all your life experiences regardless of how they felt.

Respect the power of your life and your life experiences and know you have intrinsic value that others can learn from. Share your wisdom by living a life filled with your authenticity; your truth, aliveness, joy and gratitude.

Join with others who have similar hopes and dreams for the future and brainstorm these possibilities. The power of shared visions and values creates magic beyond your expectations.

Never doubt that a small group of thoughtful
Committed citizens can change the world.
Indeed, it's the only thing that ever has.

Margaret Mead

FOCUS

- **Curiosity**

   Our children are our future. Their natural curiosity generates evolutionary thinking. This innate quality lives in you to this day. . .exercise your curiosity.

- **Innocence**

   Receptivity and acceptance are attributes of innocence, the ability to be with life and to not have to understand everything nor control it.

- **Oneness**

All life is interconnected; we all share the same breath and the same sun power. Live this truth and watch your life expand.

QUESTIONS AND GUIDELINES

1. What is your most life-transforming experience?
2. How did you feel when this event occurred in your life?
3. Do you appreciate the value of this event more now than you did at the time it occurred?
4. What words of inspiration do you have for today's youth?
5. What do you want to share with couples to encourage them in their relationship with each other?
6. Parenting is very different today than it was when you were growing up and when you were parenting. What have you learned that could be helpful for today's parents?
7. The famous question: What would you do differently in your life, given the chance?

82½ to 85 Years

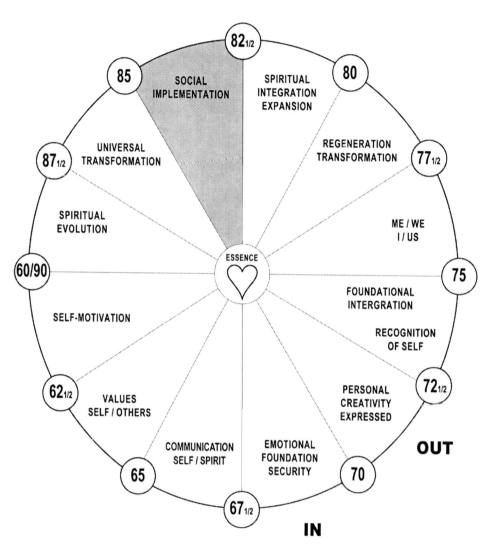

THEME

Career/ Profession
How you are seen in the world
Outlet for your creativity

Chapter 37

Public Identity

POWER

Your values in life are very expanded and different now than they were when you visited this particular cycle at 22½ to 25 (Chapter 13) or even at 52½ to 55 (Chapter 25). This cycle is focused on the way you present yourself to the world: your values, attitudes, beliefs, behavior, personality presentation, position, etc.

This time around you are able to look at the world and your part in it through the eyes of experience and the innate wisdom that lives in you. The nice part at this time in your life, there is also the recognition that you do not have to take responsibility for everything in life except you and how you personally feel and behave.

In whatever way you choose to interface with the world, through your vocation, an avocation, your hobbies, traveling or any other experience that brings you joy and meaning in your life is very important. At this age, you have the opportunity to relax into your life experiences and appreciate yourself and others in deeper, more meaningful ways.

Each time you enter this cycle and review your life, you will probably be amazed how much you have changed in your view and attitude towards yourself and life in general. Life is a process of changes and experiences and your attitude and actions determine the quality of your life as you encounter these changes. You really are in the driver's seat of choice as far as how you are going to respond to life. This is comforting and empowering so you can meet each moment of life and know that you can influence your experience by your intention and desires.

VULNERABILITY

In the western world, unlike the indigenous tribes, we usually do not use rites of passage to recognize and honor life changes. Many powerful and enduring changes in your personal experiences in life can go unrecognized because your life changs were not consciously empowered. This can create a foggy, confused condition in your life because a part of you, your heart and soul, recognizes the shift in life and your conscious mind may be trying to identify and figure out "what is going on?"

Each time you enter a new cycle in life, it is a powerful change in direction and focus, which your whole neurological and emotional system responds to naturally. Without a conscious rite of passage, the daily aspects of life become your avenues for your rite of passage and how you will experience the changes that are influencing your life. A life style rite of passage is neither as defined nor as clear a reporting system in your life as an intentional rite of passage, and yet your daily habits are generated from these changes, consciously or unconsciously.

To maintain balance in your life, your body, mind and emotions must be "moving along with life" at the same pace of your developing consciousness. Your conscious mind is the most directly influenced part of your reality by your life conditions and experiences, and as a result you develop beliefs and behaviors that help you maintain your resiliency and sense of safety. Your conscious mind may be the last one to know that your heart and soul have made changes and now your thinking, beliefs, attitudes and behavior have to "catch up." Yesterday's values and beliefs can imprison your heart and soul if you do not consciously update your personal truth and lifestyle. Greater in-depth listening to your heart and soul and taking steps of action are keys to changing your life. Living this way, you enroll the conscious mind as a director - to assist with the action and implementation of these intentions and desires.

DISCOVERIES

Your habits constitute the way you use your energy everyday and consciously or unconsciously become your rite of passage. Through these daily habits you begin to define your reality and your movement in life. If you want to consciously change your life, start changing your daily habits by taking baby steps of change. Every day do something different than you usually do and see what happens to your mind, your emotions and your body. Through your personal experience you can determine if changing your habits increases your sense of aliveness or not. Consciously involve yourself daily with choices that are focused on life and living because this regenerates your body, mind and emotions.

In a society as mobile as the American culture, the intergenerational family unit does not naturally occur anymore for many families; rarely are grandparents and grandchildren living in the same state, let alone the same city. We are now global citizens with global families connected through the nervous system of cyberspace uniting us like one big heartbeat. Americans are also a touch-deprived society. So wherever you live, someone needs a loving caring mentor or grandparent. Make yourself available to love and be loved. Everyone needs to love and be loved and without that experience life can feel empty and unfilfilled. Love is the natural law of life. The illusions that create separation are made up by human minds. Eternally we are seeking our way home to love, the truth of life that lives in our heart and soul. To love and be loved is the path of the heart to consciously unite us with our soul and each other.

DIRECTIVES

Entering this cycle again, you can consciously choose and direct your daily choices to support how you want to live your life now. How do you want to be seen, heard and recognized in the world today? This might be quite different than it was 30 or 60-years ago, so it is important to update your choices so they reflect your current values.

It is important to really appreciate the wisdom and truth that life has offered you through your personal experiences. Since you were busy "living your life" in the previous years, you may not have had time to assess and appreciate you. Now is a good time to make that assessment and determine how you want to share your love and wisdom for your benefit and the benefit for the global family. Sharing your love and wisdom, as an elder, is not making yourself responsible for others, just allowing you to show up in life in a loving way and be of service. All humans need to be in service to the children because they are our future, and without our support, they cannot possibly have a safe, loving world to live in. So when in doubt, serve the children.

This does not mean you have to begin preaching, teaching or recruiting ears to hear you; it means that life will bring to you those who could directly or indirectly benefit from your love and wisdom. It is your responsibility to be present enough in your own life with the people who come into your life, to know that your love and wisdom are gifts, and to be willing to share as the moment presents itself. Love does not need an agenda to be shared with others. These moments may cause you to look at your self-worth and self-esteem issues and accept that life is your greatest teacher and humbleness and gratitude your greatest presentation.

The whole of reality is contained in the present moment.

Deepak Chopra

FOCUS

- **Freedom of expression**

  Live your truth, walk your talk. You are a gift in life, and that gift is to be shared as you live it.

- **Individuality**

  There is no one on this planet like you. Share your heart's wisdom, even if it seems simple; what may seem simple to you may be the voice of God to another.

- **Joy**

Deep abiding joy is the direct doorway to your soul. Joy is innate and always shining within your heart to guide you home to love and truth in your daily life. Feel your JOY.

QUESTIONS AND GUIDELINES

1. Do you recognize that you are a wise one, a mentor with great wisdom gleaned from your personal life lessons and experiences? If not, why not?

2. Do you know it is a privilege for other generations to spend time with you and hear your life story?

3. Are you willing to share your love and wisdom with others?

4. What do you need to do to increase your personal joy in life?

5. List three beliefs that "hold you back" from sharing your love and wisdom with others.

6. List three qualities that you know you have that enrich your life and the lives of others.

7. Are you willing to ask for what you want from others when you need support?

85 to 87½ Years

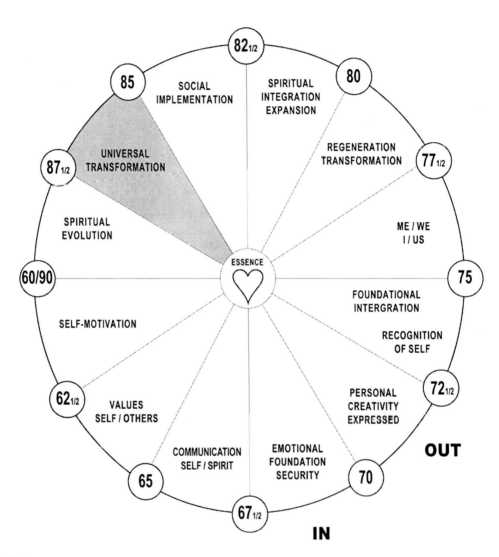

THEME

    Humanitarian needs
    Global family awareness
    Transformation

Chapter 38

Universal Awareness

POWER

From the time you went through this cycle at age 25 - 27½ (Chapter 14) and during the second time at 55 - 57½ (Chapter 26), your focus is the same at this age - pay attention to the global family, the needs of humanity and your part in it. Even though the focus is the same, each time you are in this cycle your lifestyle is probably very different. Once again it is time to look at the big picture of life: how are we functioning on this planet as a global family? Recognizing that our electronic and technological world has diminished distance and separation, no matter where we live on the earth, we are each influencing all life on this planet.

As you become consciously aware that everything is energy and information, that all life is interconnected beyond what your mind understands, then you can recognize that your heart and soul recognizes oneness as a lifestyle.

When you go to a movie, even if you just focus on the person who is speaking, at some level you are still aware of the whole scene and everything that is going on. This is how life is -- everything is going on at once and whether we know it or understand it does not change the conditions of life, only our experience. If you focus only on one part of your reality, that becomes your world of experience. You may feel isolated and alone in this reality or you may feel safe and secure.

If you focus on the big picture of life, you can participate as part of the audience and allow yourself greater objectivity and awareness on a global level. You will be amazed at how different your experience is when you perceive life from a greater vantage point. When you view life as a hologram, the needs of humanity take on a different meaning and relationship to your personal life and belief system. This allows you to be part of the solution rather than being part of the problem with emotional reactionary beliefs and behavior.

VULNERABILITY

Oneness is an inside job. All life is interconnected, and you cannot be disconnected from Oneness. It is impossible. You can create a life filled with the *experience of separation* by living with a value system that *condemns you* rather than praising and supporting you. With this kind of reality, your sense of self-worth or deserving is diminished daily so you cannot experience the blessings of your heart and soul. Through fear and judgment of yourself and others, you can cloud your mental and emotional balance which interferes with change happening naturally and causes limitations for your receiving life's blessings easily.

There is a life cycle that we seem to go through as human beings. When we are born, we are very open, receptive and spontaneous. As we grow and are imprinted and influenced by our environment and caregivers, we learn to confine ourselves to get love and approval or at the worst to avoid harm. In the continuing years, based on our personal life experiences, our confinement and loss of spontaneity will continue to increase until we forget what it really feels like to be alive, carefree and happy; when this occurs, the wonder and enchantment of life fades and we become survivalists.

We always have the opportunity to return to a state of pureness and innocence, regardless of our life experiences, because that is the naturalness of our heart and soul. As your conscious mind allows you to let go of life conditions and experiences that are minimizing and limiting you, your heart is lifted and you begin to feel more and more alive at any age.

DISCOVERIES

Everything is energy and information. Light is both a beam and a particle. You breathe in, you breathe out. For every action, there is a reaction. Even with all these principles of physics, your reality is still based on your perception developed through your life experiences. However you perceive your reality is the determining factor for the way you behave and relate to everything and everyone in your life. You have unlimited choice in your perceptual reality. You can look at your life as small and confined by the human condition, you can perceive your self as a victim in life, you can look at life as predestined, you can look at life as empty and void of substance or fulfillment and you can look at your life as a soul unfolding according to a divine plan. These are just a few ideas that you can create about your reality. With six billion people on this planet, we probably have six billion realities playing all the time, and your reality is unique unto you.

Since everything is energy and information, movement and change make it possible for life to be evolving. You have seen many changes in your lifetime, some that bring a glow to your heart as you remember them and some that can cause you to have tears in your eyes. Life is a hologram and every experience contributes to this moment and who you are right now. How do you want your life to be today and for the rest of your life? The choices that you make today will determine what tomorrow looks like and feels like in your reality.

Because this cycle is so expansive and calling you into your global awareness, which may or may not be comfortable for you, the more open minded you can be, the easier it is to move with these dramatic changes in your daily life. There are a lot of things that you may worry about that you are discovering don't matter as much now as they did when you were younger. You can also be taking on more worry in different ways than you did earlier in your life.

Your comfort in this cycle is based on your ability to accept life as an infinite possibility. That does not mean that you have to understand everything in your life or anyone else's nor agree with life's conditions. Acceptance is a blanket of grace and offers you the key to living in the moment, right where your feet and your heart live. When your mind is present,. in this moment, you make the choice of how you will feel and relate to the people, places and things in your life right now.

DIRECTIVES

If you look at your life movie as an observer or part of the audience and recognize the different roles you have played, then you have a different vantage point of your life experience. You can review your life movie through the eyes of a critic, looking for what is missing or what is wrong with your movie, possibly causing you to feel sad and judgmental of yourself. You can also choose to review your life movie as a work of art--completely unique, powerful, challenging and creative--and feel deep gratitude and appreciation for all that you have been through and created throughout your life. The choice is yours and it will determine the quality of every day of your life. This cycle provides another moment of choice for your life: *expansion*.

Make your world bigger by thinking bigger and feeling the value of your personal life. You can reclaim the wonder and enchantment of your childhood and your heart's desires, or you can choose to live with limitation and confinement, which can create a bleak and hopeless world, lacking any sense of aliveness. It is that clear and powerful. You *can* choose how you will relate to your life conditions and experiences that influence your aliveness and joy, no matter your age or your physical mobility.

FOCUS

* **Interconnectedness**

   All life on the planet is inter-dependent… we need each other to make the circle of life complete and workable. Accept your part in the divine plan of creation.

* **Big Picture**

   In the big picture of life, your problems become smaller. In a small picture of life, your problems or challenges can feel like they become bigger than you are. Think and focus on the big picture of life and your place in it will feel more balanced.

* **Allowing**

   You deserve to relax and enjoy your life in comfort, inside and out. Allow yourself to accept this gift and know that you deserve this support.

QUESTIONS AND GUIDELINES

1. What happens to your heart and your joy when you look at your life from the small picture?

2. What happens to your heart and your joy when you look at your life from the big picture?

3. Look at three scenes in your life movie that need to blessed and released by forgiving yourself or others. Enfold these situations in the Light and allow love to provide the release for everyone involved.

4. Give yourself permission to release suffering, pain, struggle, and limitation, embrace peace, relaxation, joy, worthiness, faith, and trust in yourself and others.

5. List six things that create a quality lifestyle for you. They can be possessions, places, people, emotions, etc.

6. List three things you want in your life right now that will increase your joy and aliveness.

87½ to 90 Years

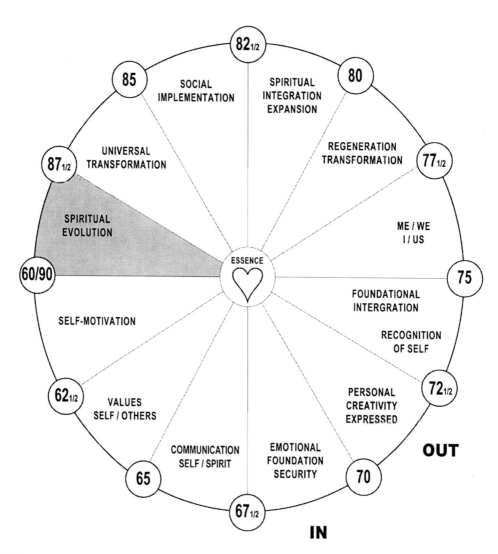

THEME

Inner renewal
Spiritual regeneration
Personal inventory

Chapter 39

Spiritual Foundation

POWER

Y̲ou are an earth angel. Your consciousness continues to expand, in ever-widening circles of awareness so that you have no veils that separate you from the truth of your heart and soul and the universal wisdom. You do not have to "keep track of meaningless details of life" in the way you used to. Someone else can manage that right now. You are on duty as an earth angel to live closely with love, life and spirit as one voice and share that wisdom and peace with the world, just by living.

You are born in a world of oneness and you return to the world of oneness when you allow yourself to listen, see and hear the voice of the universe through your heart and soul. Love is your true "home." You can live in oneness while still in a body. That is exactly what our babies teach us by their presence and that is also possible for you as well. When you live in harmony with your inner world, your outer world becomes a daily reflection of that depth of life that is possible when you stay open to your heart and soul, your inner wisdom.

VULNERABILITY

You may sense a certain vulnerability at this age and in this cycle particularly, because your mental and spiritual ability to interface with more than one reality is very accessible right now. This is the cycle of spiritual transformation and your access to your intuition and inner awareness is as easy as answering the telephone when it rings. This connection takes place inside of you. It is not new. You were born with this deep inner connection to spirit and the universal principles andit is being highly activated right now.

Your vulnerability in this cycle is based on your willingness to trust yourself. By now, you know that what you see and hear in your inner world may be very different in the outer world and you do not have to understand the difference. Trust is the bridge that supports your life as a spiritual being living in a human body.

DISCOVERIES

This is such a special cycle when you re-enter the spiritual womb, the inner world of your soul, and allow a new life to emerge through you. You can be free from the past and any conditions or limitations you may have created for yourself through your beliefs or life experiences. This is the time to be "born again," living in the same body and yet having a whole new outlook on life as seen through the eyes of your heart and soul which is free of rose-colored glasses or the world of denial. When you accept life just as it is, you can relax and enjoy your life, one breath at a time, one day at a time. You recognize the quality of life because you have had many years to participate in many ways and gain great wisdom.

You are a messenger through which life can share wisdom and creativity with everyone you meet. This receptivity is a childlike quality that we love so much in the children. It naturally emerges through you again during this cycle. This quality lives in all of us forever; it just gets buried by all the details, illusions, drama, and hurt of human existence. It is instantly renewed when you allow spirit to flow through your heart into the world as love and acceptance and gratitude for all life.

DIRECTIVES

Whether you choose to live another 30 minutes, 30 days or 30 years, what really matters is the quality of your relationship with your heart and soul and how you share the love that you are with the world. This is the focus for life and it is increased naturally in this cycle. The relationship with your heart and soul is the longest-term relationship you have had your whole entire life, and it continues forever. You are your own *soul mate* and when you allow your heart and soul to be your guiding force in your life, your sense of deep abiding love and peace is infinite. When you intimately relate with consciousness through your heart and soul, the world is created differently from your perception every moment of every day.

This cycle is the call to re-engage once again in your daily life, with these childlike qualities of spontaneity, curiosity, innocence and joy. When you agree to meet each day with these qualities, you become a "blank canvas" on which your heart and soul can create new life, vibrantly alive and filled with wonder. Even if you do not feel your childlike wonder in life, it does not mean wonder has gone away; it is simply waiting for you to reclaim it and summon it to aliveness through your joy. The call is yours, and these wondrous childlike qualities are awaiting your recognition, no matter how long they have been hidden. It is never too late to have a happy childhood and share your joy with the world. You are the gift to life and we celebrate you.

FOCUS

- **Love**

  Live everyday, in love with life, in love with all that you are in life and all that life brings to you daily. Live your life through love.

- **Rejoice**

  Today is 24 hours of life - REJOICE that you are here seeing, breathing and gifting life with your Presence as well as being blessed by living.

- **Gratitude**

  Receive all life experiences in gratitude. Somewhere in the Universal Plan all life is coherent and in divine order, and you are a unique part of that plan.

QUESTIONS AND GUIDELINES

1. What does your heart and soul desire in life at this time?

2. What kind of support do you need and want in order to take steps of action to fulfill your desire?

3. Do you have a dream or a vision that you have believed in or desired since you were a child?

4. How can you begin to create that dream or vision?

5. Have you shared this vision and asked for support from your angels and others to create it?

6. Name 3 gifts that you have to give to others.

7. Name 3 gifts that you want given to you.

8. Do you recognize what a gift you are to life and those who know and love you?

Chapter 40

Fourth Thirty-Year Cycle

90 to Forever

Divine Wisdom - at the age of 90, entering this Thirty-Year cycle for the fourth time, longevity itself is a major and admirable quality of life. People are curious and interested in what you think; they want to know about your history. Your life is intriguing to them because your vantage point in life spans such a long time and has involved many changes, including inventions that may have occurred before they were even born. The veil of consciousness gets thinner and thinner during this cycle, and it is easier to be a part of the spiritual world and still be in a body. Since your personal willfulness has had many years of expression, your willingness to receive Spirit gracefully and allow your innate wisdom to come through you is fulfilling and gratifying for you and those who are blessed to receive what you share.

FROM 90 TO . . . forever

LOVE AND APPRECIATE YOURSELF

AND

DO WHATEVER YOU WANT TO DO

THAT BRINGS YOU JOY AND ALIVENESS.

BLESSINGS TO YOU,

Kay

Other Books by Sage Publishers

Point of Power: A Relationship with Your Soul by Kay Snow-Davis
POINT OF POWER is a simple and reliable method you can reference to recognize your natural creativity and abilities which enhances every aspect of your life; relating to yourself and others without judgment and greater appreciation and respect.

Wheel of Life Cycles: The Power of Love to Heal Your Life by Kay Snow-Davis
There is no other person in life that sees and lives in the world the way you do. You are the producer, director and star of your life movie. You can change the experiences in your life by changing your perception.

Gateways to the Soul: Heart of Astrology by Kay Snow-Davis & Margaret Koolman
Astrology is an ancient window for navigation with the universe. Find and recognize your personal Gateways to your soul commitments in this powerful work.

Other Publications

Wake-up…Live the Life You Love with Kay Snow-Davis and other talented authors:
Deepak Chopra, Wayne Dryer, and Mark Victor Hansen
Finding purpose and living with passion is the main stake of abundance. Learn how the authors overcame hardship, found their purpose and passion and are now living productive, abundance-filled lives and are sharing their lessons, success and happiness.

Other Products and Services from Global Family Education Center

Point of Power CD Set: This one-hour audio overview of Point Of Power gives you the qualities of each modality - Root, Trunk, Branch and Leaf. This is great listening to boost your self-confidence and recognition of your creativity.

Wheel of Life CD, English and Japanese: Take an audio life journey of the first 30 years of your life and see you and your life experiences with new eyes – healing is inevitable.

Point of Power and Wheel of Life Tele-seminars: Any time, any place you can tune in and have expanded guidelines for greater recognition and appreciation of you, your partner, your family, your co-workers. Working together creates balanced living.

Generational Cycles CD, English and Japanese: Life is bigger than our beliefs and experiences. Expand your awareness in this audio presentation and recognize and embrace your collective soul commitment with the generation you were born into.

Soul Purpose Astrology Sessions: Are you seeking your life purpose? Do you feel like there is something special for you to express in your life? This service provides a map for your soul so you can become conscious of your soul commitments.

Soul Purpose Astrology Consultations: Do you want to have a cutting edge in today's world of business? Recognize and use the power of your company through cooperation with the Universal Principles and stabilize and advance your influence in the world.

Soul Purpose Astrologer Certification: We live in a unified field, recognized by Einstein years ago. Take advantage of this power, become a certified SPA astrologer, and offer your wisdom and power through the Universal tool of astrology.

Kau'ai Retreats: Now is the time in life to enter the inner vision quest of your life and discover your creativity, wisdom and joy, in service to life and the planet. Kau'ai is the perfect place to retreat into your self and discover your beauty and power.

International Trainings and Seminars: All of our services are available to be specifically designed to suit your personal, family, corporate or national needs. Please contact us so we can co- create the support that you desire.

www.GlobalFamilyEducation.com
www.GFEC.com
info@GFEC.com

About the Author

Kay Snow-Davis is an International Author, Soul Purpose Astrologer, and Inspirational Speaker. Her innate wisdom and knowledge in the field of personal and spiritual development is extensive and advanced. Through her varied life experiences and deep inner quest for life's meaning, Kay has developed a unique and powerful model of Life Mentoring, based on Universal principles and indigenous wisdom and values.

She has been actively involved in the Human Potential Movement for over 35 years and has participated as founder or co-founder of several corporations in the US, all associated with spiritual, humanistic development. She is founder and president of Global Family Education Center, Inc.

Her model of Life Mentoring has influenced many personal and professional lives internationally, recently including Japan and China. She has consulted with a vast array of international clientele and corporations, including financial and investment firms, medical practitioners, chiropractic and dental practices, real estate and construction companies, public and alternative school programs, adolescent treatment programs, family mentoring programs, prisons, disaster recovery programs, youth at risk, crisis coordinator trainings and trauma specialist seminars.

She is a mother, grandmother, foster mother and "Aunty" to her personal family and her extended family. Her passion is, *"make this world safe for our children, they are our future, and we must support them"*.

Ms. Snow-Davis is the author of ***Point of Power: A Relationship With Your Soul*** and ***Wheel of Life Cycles: The Power of Love to Heal Your Life.*** She is co-author, with an English astrologer, Margaret Koolman, of ***Gateways to the Soul: Heart of Astrology****, to be published in 2007.*

Contact information:

ksd@GlobalFamilyEducation.com

For more information on personal, family or group sessions, seminars, trainings, corporate consultations, or teacher certification you may contact:

Global Family Education Center, Inc

Box 60

Kapa'a, Kau'ai, Hawaii 96746

808.822.4332 VM

808.822.9877 Fax

info@GlobalFamilyEducation.com

Websites:

www.GlobalFamilyEducation.com

www.WheelOfLifeCycles.com

www.GFEC.com

www.SoulPurposeAcademy.com

www.KaySnow-Davis.com

Referral Websites:

Neurological Clearing and Pain Management

Dr. Art Karno
www.KarnoPrinciple.com

Dr. Jae Atchley
www.UniversalHealthMethod.com

Dr. Stephen Daniel
www.QuantumTechniques.com

Gary Craig
www.EmoFree.com